Life on the Tenure Track

W9-AQS-203

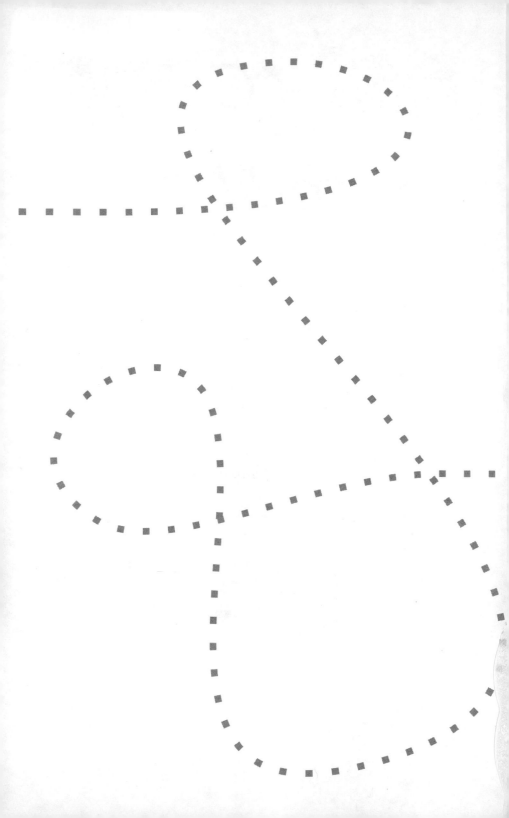

Life
on the
Tenure
Track

Lessons from  the First Year

James M. Lang

The Johns Hopkins University Press
Baltimore and London

© 2005 The Johns Hopkins University Press
All rights reserved. Published 2005
Printed in the United States of America on acid-free paper
2 4 6 8 9 7 5 3 1

The Johns Hopkins University Press
2715 North Charles Street
Baltimore, Maryland 21218-4363
www.press.jhu.edu

Library of Congress Cataloging-in-Publication Data

Lang, James M.
Life on the tenure track : lessons from the first year /
James M. Lang.
p.   cm.
ISBN 0-8018-8102-1 (hardcover : alk. paper) —
ISBN 0-8018-8103-X (pbk. : alk. paper)
1. Teachers—Tenure—United States. 2. First year teachers—
United States. 3. College teachers—United States. I. Title.
LB2836.L36 2005
378.1'214—dc22   2004021143

A catalog record for this book is available from the
British Library.

For Anna Mae Lang,
my first and favorite teacher, whose impression on me becomes
more apparent and more welcome with each passing year

Contents

Preface

To write about an entire year of one's life, no matter how closely the writer wishes to maintain his fidelity to the truth, requires a good deal of selecting and shaping. I can't write about everything that happened to me, so I have to identify the events that stand out in my mind and that seem most relevant for others in my position—or wanting to be in my position.

As I look back over the year and try to reconstruct so many days and weeks and months from both documents and memory, invariably the events that stand out most clearly are the ones that were especially traumatic or puzzling. Those were the events that I continued to reflect on long after the year had ended and that still stand out in my mind now, three years later.

Because the book focuses on many of these intensely felt experiences, the more satisfying and pleasant—but often mundane—moments of life on the tenure track may get lost in the narrative or subsumed under the weight of my anxiety stories. But those ordinary moments of contentment played a major role in my life during that year, and I have tried to highlight them when I could.

Still, as anyone who has read Dante's *Divine Comedy* will attest, hell makes for more interesting stories than heaven. To the reader for whom my time in the inferno leaves the more permanent impression than my time in paradise, I would point out that I remain on the tenure track, three years later, a satisfied and fulfilled member of the faculty, hoping for the tenure decision that will secure my job here. I know the answers now to many of the questions I asked in my first year; I am more familiar with the landmarks and guideposts in the often confusing territory through which I blundered so blindly.

Preface

The selection and shaping required by the narrative form requires no apology and minimal explanation in a nonfiction narrative. But a second element that has some role to play in my fidelity to the truth of my experiences deserves a fuller explanation.

In this book I have written about friends, colleagues, supervisors, and students. I have done my best to convey my impressions of them *during my first year*. In many cases those impressions have changed during the subsequent two and a half years. For example, I know now that I perhaps overestimated the number of faculty members at the college who taught by lecture alone, as I describe in the September chapter. I understand a little more clearly now why the college's president takes the time to have a personal meeting, however brief, with all new faculty members, as I describe in the October chapter. And while at the time it seemed as if the clocks, TVs, and VCRs in my classrooms were always broken, I probably remember only the broken ones and have forgotten about all the ones that worked. At any rate, the college has undergone substantial physical improvements since that first year of mine, and the modern classrooms I teach in now look very different from those first ones.

Enumerating all the ways in which my perspective has changed from my first year would take another book entirely. I'll save those impressions for the sequel. But no one should take my portraits of the characters in this story or the college itself as either *my* final word or *the* final word on them. The people in this story would surely tell very different stories about themselves and their places in the world, and I acknowledge the validity of their stories. Three years later, I would have different stories to tell about them as well.

Because I wanted the book to contain plenty of detail and description, I did not bother trying to mask the identity of the college, nor did I want to distort substantially the identities of the people with whom I spent a lot of time—my departmental colleagues. I believe I have not described them in ways that would make them want to disown my portraits of them.

It was easy enough, though, to mask people's identities for readers outside the college; I had only to change first names and to omit last names. I felt this was important because some of our professional obligations require working with editors, grant-funding agencies, and teachers at other universities, and I did not want to interfere with my colleagues' ability to conduct that part of their professional lives without prejudice.

I worked a little harder to protect the identities of students and the job candidates I discuss in chapter 6. In those cases I did my best to erase any distinguishing marks, even occasionally changing their gender or altering their physical appearance and background. I modified people's identities only in ways that did not change the character of my interaction with them or alter the specific story I had to tell about them. Aside from my own departmental colleagues, then, readers should not imagine that they see themselves reflected perfectly in this book, because no one appears here exactly as in real life.

With all of these qualifiers, I have still told the truth about my first year on the tenure track as openly and honestly as I can. I have not created any composite or fictional characters; I have not interjected events from later years into my first year; and I have not omitted anything significant that happened during that first year. As a writer of nonfiction, I believe that people engaged in this enterprise have an obligation to remain faithful to the truth of their experiences without causing unnecessary complications in the lives of the people they write about.

I have done my best to keep that faith.

Acknowledgments

In the spring of 2004 I was elected by the senior class at Assumption College to give the Baccalaureate address. The students who selected me for that honor are the very students with whom I had failed so miserably in my first days and weeks as a teacher. I am first grateful to those students for sticking with me, as I stuck with them, for giving me the opportunity to teach them and to learn from them, and for their contributions to my courses and their support of me as a faculty member.

As for the book itself, Emily Toth was the first person to nudge me towards writing it, and I probably would never have undertaken it without her advice and encouragement. I am very grateful for her help.

Mike Land has read early drafts of every column I have written for the *Chronicle of Higher Education* and early versions of many chapters in this book. His editorial suggestions, and his generosity with his time, have made this a better book than it otherwise would have been.

Rachel Ramsey has also read early drafts of many *Chronicle* columns and early versions of chapters in this book. She has been one of the most unflagging supporters of my writing, and many times in moments of doubt my confidence has been renewed by her response to my work.

I am grateful to the English department at Assumption College for helping to make my first year as good as it could have been, especially Cora Castaldi, who made me feel very welcome upon my arrival. I thank Dana Aspinall and Dave Thoreen for their friendship and advice during that year. I am grateful as well to the members of the senior administration of Assumption College, who have supported my writing and my career in various ways, including Dean Mary Lou Anderson, former Provost Joe Gower, and President Tom Plough.

The debt I owe to Ken Bain for helping me begin my career on the tenure track successfully should be clear from the book itself, so to Ken I offer simply my thanks.

I am grateful to my two editors at the *Chronicle of Higher Education*, first Liz McMillen and now Denise Magner, for starting me down the road of writing about academic life and for allowing me to continue my journey along it.

My family have provided me with their love and support as always, and they know how much it has meant to me.

An anonymous reader of the first draft of the manuscript offered immensely helpful suggestions, which spurred some valuable revisions of the book.

Mary Yates's copyediting made me a far better writer in this book than I am in real life.

Finally and especially I wish to acknowledge Jackie Wehmueller, who has proved a wise and friendly editor, one with whom any writer should count him- or herself fortunate to work.

Life on the
Tenure Track

Before (and After)
the Beginning

In late December 1996, I was sitting in a bar in Washington, D.C., with
five or six other graduate students from the English department at Northwestern University. We were sharing horror stories about the four-day
convention from which we were momentarily escaping, the annual meeting of the Modern Language Association.

I remember sipping slowly at a beer, gazing at the graffiti-splashed
walls of the bar, and feeling like one of the lucky ones. Unlike several of
my colleagues, I had managed to land the prize we had all traveled to our
nation's capital in search of: a job interview.

That was the source of my pride and self-satisfaction at the major
conference for my field, where English and modern-language professors
from around the world come to exchange their latest ideas, and to interview graduate students for job openings in their departments. Graduate
students from top universities, with cutting-edge dissertation topics,
bustle between the convention hotels from one interview to the next,
dearly purchased interview suits rumpling as the day wears on. I have
heard of job-seekers cramming a dozen or more interviews into the convention's four days.

And me?

Well, I had managed to secure an interview. One interview. For a replacement position. Outside of my field. One year, no chance of renewal.
At a small university in northern Ohio.

The awful part was that in some ways I had reason to be proud, at least
in relation to my barroom colleagues who had come up empty-handed.
Most of them were further along in their dissertations than I was, and

I

several had more marketable dissertation topics and vastly more teaching experience than I did.

And if my pride in that one interview wasn't already embarrassing enough, it turned out that I wasn't even a finalist for the job. Later that year, though, another opportunity arose. I had spent some time that academic year—my final one as a graduate student—helping out at Northwestern's Searle Center for Teaching Excellence, which sponsored lectures, conducted workshops, and pursued research on teaching and learning in higher education. My role was to work with the director in developing programs for teaching assistants while the center conducted a search for an assistant director who would assume those responsibilities full-time.

In the late spring I became aware that my name had been entered into the list of candidates for that position; in the early summer the director of the center offered me the job. In addition to the work I would be doing with teaching assistants, the position offered me the opportunity to teach one course per year for the English department and the chance to pursue research and publish articles on teaching and learning.

Perhaps equally important, the three-year contract offered me and my wife, Anne—and our one-year-old baby—something we desperately wanted: the chance for some stability, for two steady incomes, for a house, and for the continued pleasures of life in Chicago. So I took the job and became a full-time employee at Northwestern on September 1, 1997, four days after having submitted my final dissertation to the graduate school.

I found the work at the Searle Center fascinating and fulfilling. I spent a good deal of time observing graduate students and faculty from all disciplines in the classroom, talking with them about their ideas on teaching in particular and education in general. That work gave me an incredibly broad perspective on the enterprise of higher education, and I found that I very much enjoyed reflecting upon the teaching and learning that went on in disciplines and programs far removed from my own. That cross-fertilization of ideas and the interdisciplinary nature of the work—the sometimes startling new perspectives on the teaching of literature that I got from studying the teaching of physics, for example—made my first two years at the center intellectually challenging and satisfying.

Which is not to say that I never thought about pursuing the tenure-track position I had been dreaming of since graduate school. In my first year at the center I applied for one job and made it as far as the on-campus interview for a tenure-track position at a college in South Carolina. I felt that the interview went well, but when I left the English department office at the end of the day I saw a notice posted by the faculty mailboxes announcing the departmental meeting at which the English faculty would cast their votes for me or the other candidate. I remember thinking how impossible it seemed that I could have been impressive enough to sway an entire department to vote for me—and my fears were confirmed when I received the phone call two weeks later telling me I had not been the first choice. It felt as if a golden opportunity had slipped through my fingers.

The following year a different opportunity arose, this time at a college in downtown Chicago, which was looking to hire a director for its newly established teaching center. I would be the founding director of this teaching center at the tender age of twenty-nine. I wasn't sure I really wanted the position, but I certainly wanted better pay for the work I was doing and hoped I could get that either from the new college or as a result of a counteroffer from Northwestern. The director of the Searle Center had once told me that as far as he could tell, the only way people ever got a substantial raise in big research universities was when they received outside job offers and the university was forced to counteroffer. So I applied for this new position, interviewed, and did indeed receive an offer that would have substantially improved my salary.

That offer prompted some serious soul-searching, the result of which was the conviction that I was not yet prepared to give up the dream of obtaining a regular faculty position in English. Accepting that job as director of the teaching center would have meant taking another step down an administrative path from which it would have been increasingly difficult to turn back.

Turning down that appointment was a decision I rethought on a weekly basis for the next year. One of the best moments of my life had been standing under an elevated train track outside an expensive restaurant in downtown Chicago, the ground covered with snow and ice, just out of a dinner with eight faculty members and deans from that college—several of whom had challenged me with contentious questions—hearing the dean in charge of the job search tell me how wonderfully I had performed and that she would be calling me with an offer the following morning. One of the worst moments of my life was having to call her back a week later and turn down a permanent position in Chicago and a $10,000-a-year raise in exchange for the pursuit of the impossible dream that next fall: a tenure-track position in my field.

But once I had made that awful phone call, my course was set. Anne and I agreed that this was the time—the fall of 1999—for me to head back into the market for tenure-track jobs in English, and that it was now or never. I would give myself one, perhaps two years on the market. If nothing panned out, I would try to settle in and move my way up the administrative ladder at Northwestern.

In the summer of that year, as I was slowly beginning to update my curriculum vitae and hack away at drafts of cover letters, the Northwestern English department listserv passed along an e-mail message that had been sent to graduate students at a number of research universities across the nation from an editor of the online edition of the *Chronicle of Higher Education*. The magazine was looking for writers who would publish essays about their experiences on the job market that year in the Career Network pages of the *Chronicle*'s website. Anyone who was interested was instructed to write a sample first column and submit it to the editor named in the message.

This call for writers appealed to me. I was one of those people—and we are legion—who entered graduate school in English because I had long harbored ambitions to write the Great American Novel and didn't particularly want to work in a regular job. I imagined I would hang out in graduate school until my writing career took off and then become a full-time writer, churning out bestselling literary fictions from my apartment in Greenwich Village, knocking off at noon like Hemingway and whiling away the rest of the day drinking red wine on my balcony.

That dream didn't quite pan out. After six years in graduate school, I'd had less than a handful of creative writing pieces accepted in *very* obscure literary magazines, which either paid me with a free copy of the magazine or folded between the time they accepted my work and the time it was scheduled to appear. Meanwhile, the Great American Novel—which

I did work very diligently on—always seemed to be about twenty pages and one more revision away from completion.

However, I found that I had actually become interested in the study of English literature as a discipline and in teaching at the college level. So now, eight years later, while I still dreamed of becoming a prominent figure in the American literary canon, I also wanted to be an academic superstar. Now I imagined myself not just as a novelist with a substantial body of work but as the author of a few high-powered books of literary theory, being chauffeured around Raleigh-Durham in Stanley Fish's Jaguar as he courted me to become the newest divinity in the pantheon of Duke University's English department.

It seemed to me, then, that the *Chronicle* was offering me a golden opportunity. Writing for the *Chronicle* would allow me to use at least some of my creative writing skills—such as they were at that time—and would put them in the service of writing about higher education.

The editors at the *Chronicle* liked the column I submitted, and so I set about applying for jobs and writing about the process. Because of my religious background (Catholic), my work at the Searle Center, and my wish to pursue my creative writing, I decided that the ideal school for me would be a Catholic, teaching-focused, liberal arts college. The modest research expectations at such a school, I reasoned, would allow me the time and space to pursue both academic and creative writing. And lo and behold, several Catholic liberal arts colleges were among the dozen schools that had openings in my scholarly field (post–World War II British literature) and were in the northeastern quadrant of the United States (the geographical range in which Anne and I had agreed I would concentrate my job search).

When the initial interview process had shaken out, I had two campus interviews scheduled: one at Assumption College, a Catholic liberal arts college in central Massachusetts, and another at a comprehensive university in the upper Midwest. Assumption made me the first offer, and since I had found there precisely the kind of school I was looking for, I canceled my second interview and accepted the job.

I was very happy to report this news in the final column I wrote for the *Chronicle* that year; it had occurred to me on more than one occasion that if I failed in this job search, it was going to be a *very* public failure. I had toyed with the idea of drafting a face-saving column in which I explained that I really didn't want a job anyway, and the whole thing had been some kind of sociological experiment on my part. Fortunately, that column turned out to be unnecessary.

In June, after I had written my last column and we had begun to make plans for our cross-country move from Chicago to Worcester, Massachusetts, I realized that writing those columns had been the most enjoyable aspect of that entire year. I loved having the freedom to write in a more conversational style than was permitted in scholarly work, and I found that I very much enjoyed writing about academic life. I had even received a few e-mails from graduate students at universities around the country who said that my published thoughts or advice had been useful to them in one way or another.

The more I thought about it, the more I realized how much I would miss writing that column. So I asked my editor whether she had ever considered publishing a column about life on the tenure track, offering an insider's account of the challenges facing a junior faculty member. To my surprise and delight, she replied that she had been contemplating just such a column, and she invited me to write it. We informally agreed that I would write a handful of columns per year, describing my life on the tenure track, until my tenure bid in 2006.

By the time you read this, I will have been writing for the *Chronicle* for going on five and a half years, counting my first year of columns as a job-seeker. I have not stopped enjoying them, and I have not—as I once suspected might happen—come close to running out of topics and experiences in the life of a junior professor that merit public discussion and reflection.

Near the end of my second year of writing for the *Chronicle,* my first on the tenure track, I received an e-mail from a reader whose opening paragraph caught my attention: "I have been following your story in the First Person articles for a long time . . . I am faced with a choice that I believe you might be able to give me some insight on." She had been offered an administrative position very similar to the one in which I had started my career, but she too did not want to give up her dream of a tenure-track job. She wanted to know whether I thought she should take the job.

Her message surprised me, for two reasons. First, I had not imagined that people were actually following my story, as she mentioned in the first sentence; I assumed that people looked at the job pages when they needed jobs and might happen on a column while they were printing out the ads. The second surprise was that she thought I would be able to give her career advice. I had been dispensing advice in my columns all along, of course, and it had been well received on an occasion or two, but I had never pictured myself as any sort of authority or in a position to actually advise anyone to *do* anything. But here was someone asking for advice on one of the most significant life decisions she would ever make. I wrote back and told her I thought she should take the job, based on my experience—and belief—that academic career paths are forged by jumping on just such unexpected opportunities, making the most of them, and using them to advance to new levels.

The incident started me thinking more seriously than I had done before about the readers of my columns. Was I in fact helping anyone with my stories and with the occasional advice I doled out?

Over the course of the next academic year, my second on the tenure track, the idea for this book began to germinate. Whether or not I had wise and useful advice to offer, I saw that chronicling my adventures on the tenure track (which often seem to me completely idiosyncratic) and my solutions to the problems I have encountered (which always seem to me cobbled-together and provisional) could, at the very least, prove useful in stimulating debate about the working conditions of junior faculty, about the dilemmas we all face as faculty members, and about academic life in general.

The book, thus conceived, came to fruition the following year, at the end of 2003.

I tell you all this—the story of how this book came to be—to help explain the shape and scope of the book itself. The book was initially conceived as an expanded version of the stories I had written in my four years of columns for the *Chronicle*. But a subsequent decision to focus on my first year meant that I would be able to make limited use of the *Chronicle* columns I had already written. Though you will find bits and pieces of those columns scattered throughout the narrative, most of what you are reading here has been newly written for this book.

But while the book focuses on the adventures of my first year on the tenure track, I wrote it during my fourth year. I didn't want to sacrifice the opportunity to note occasionally how my perspective on those adventures had evolved three years down the road. For this reason you will find scattered parenthetical comments that answer questions I was asking myself at that time, or that look into the future with more prescience than God has in fact seen fit to grant me. The time gap also gave me enough distance to laugh at myself a little more heartily than I would have been able to do had I written the book in the summer after my first year.

Chronologically, the book begins in August 2000 and ends in August 2001; each chapter tells the story of a month in that year. Structuring the narrative as a detailed account of my first year in this way did create a special challenge: I had to reconstruct not only events that took place as long as three years ago, but also my thoughts and feelings about those events. I did not keep a diary or journal of any sort during that year, so I had to find other ways to reconstruct it.

Fortunately, at least when it comes to anything I write, I am a packrat. So when I started poking around my computer, my office, my basement, my shelves, I realized that the task of reconstruction would not be as difficult as I had imagined. I saved all of the e-mails I sent during that year and many of the ones I received; I have notes and agendas from all departmental and college meetings; I have the lesson plans for every class I taught; I have my date book; and, of course, I have my *Chronicle* columns. I also have the friends and colleagues who lived through that year with me, and I consulted them frequently; Mark and I spent fifteen minutes one afternoon reconstructing the seating arrangements for the hiring meeting I describe in the January chapter. Cross-checking these sources against my own memories, I am confident that I have reconstructed my first year as truthfully as is possible in an imperfect human world.

My two primary audiences for the book are my fellow junior faculty members in all disciplines, especially those in their first year, and the graduate students around the country who would like to become my fellow junior faculty members. I hope I have depicted life as a first-year faculty member in a way that will help graduate students both decide whether they want this life and be better prepared for it should they choose to pursue it. I believe that other junior faculty will find a measure

of interest, and solace, in the opportunity to compare their experiences with mine, to learn from my mistakes, and to realize that they do not toil in these fields in isolation.

I had another audience in mind, though, too: senior faculty and administrators. While senior faculty by definition, and administrators more often than not, were once junior faculty, working conditions in the academy are in constant flux and have shifted in major ways over the last few decades. My senior and administrative colleagues will surely remember from their own time as junior faculty that we are always speaking to you on our guard. You are unlikely ever to get the complete truth about our experiences and emotions from those whose fate you hold in your hands. I am offering here an unguarded perspective, in the hopes that it might provoke useful discussions and conversations between junior faculty and their senior colleagues.

With these audiences in mind, I tried to convey in each chapter what I felt I have learned, from my current perspective, about some aspect of life as a junior faculty member teaching at an American college today. One or two of those lessons may be particular to teaching at a liberal arts college, but I know from conversations with friends who have landed jobs at other kinds of universities, and from the regular e-mails I receive from readers of my *Chronicle* columns, that most of these lessons have relevance to my colleagues at all different kinds of institutions.

Finally, you are not exactly holding in your hands a guidebook, though I hope you will find some guidance here. This is a story, the narrative of a single year in my life as a junior faculty member. As both a writer and a teacher of narrative, I believe that the lessons that remain most deeply implanted within us, and that have the strongest capacity to influence our behavior, are the ones we encounter in stories.

I hope you—my colleagues in academia around the country—find some useful lessons in mine.

Beginning

First Day of Teaching: Tuesday, August 29, 2000. The first day of teaching kicks off at around 7 A.M.

I am every bit as nervous as you would expect me to be. I wake, shower, help make breakfast for my two daughters, have some orange juice, pace around the house.

Anne has managed to find only a part-time job in the local school system, working as a tutor from nine to noon every day. While she is not happy about this—she wanted a full-time teaching position—it means that on Tuesdays and Thursdays, my two teaching days in the fall semester, she can get the girls ready in the morning and take Madeleine (age two) to daycare and Katie (age four) to kindergarten. I am free, at least for today, to concentrate on getting through a day I have been imagining for half a year now, since I received my job offer in February.

I leave the house at 7:45 and am in my office before 8:00. We lucked into a house just two miles from campus, so I have an easy commute. Copies of my syllabi are stacked on an empty bookshelf, and the lesson plans I have been laboring over for weeks are organized in separate folders for each class. All papers are neat and tidy. I am wearing a coat and tie; have been to the bathroom four times in twenty minutes; review the schedule in my date book one last, unnecessary time:

8:30–9:45:	Freshman Composition
11:30–12:45:	Contemporary British Fiction
1:30–2:30:	Office Hour
2:30–3:45:	Freshman Composition

I fill a glass with water, gather up my course materials, and walk to a nearby building on a sunny late-summer morning. Eight hours, I keep telling myself. In eight hours it will all be over, and you will have finished your first day of teaching and can look back on it with satisfaction. You just have to get through the next eight hours.

Into the Kennedy Building, room 06, the classroom I had scoped out a few days before. It's a nondescript brick building, built during the 1950s, boxy and modernist. My classroom is a plain rectangle, white brick walls, two blackboards, no air conditioning. Crucifix on the upper back wall of the room, as in every other room on campus, and a broken clock. The door is at the rear of the room. I move through the rows of desks and up to the front, set my stuff down on the big desk, and look up to face my students.

First Day I Felt Like an English Professor. I first felt like an assistant professor of English literature on a day when the opening of the semester was still a few weeks off. My exploration of Assumption's small campus—175 acres of hilly and wooded terrain, with buildings and open green areas spaced nicely throughout—had led me to the recreation center, where the student-athletes were training. I spent a half-hour there on an exercise bike.

Sweaty and exhausted, I went in search of a drinking fountain and passed a group of students and coaches for some athletic team sitting on lounge chairs in the lobby. I couldn't help but overhear their conversation. They were trying to remember the name of a famous novel they had read, all of them throwing out what little bits of it they could recall.

"It was at a boarding school," said one.

"Yeah, the guy's name was Gene," said another.

"And Phineas—that was his friend. And one of them fell out of a tree."

"What was that book?"

"I think it was a Charles Dickens novel."

"Is it *David Copperfield?*"

I couldn't help myself; they were nearly a century off. I tossed the answer over my shoulder. "*A Separate Peace,*" I said. "John Knowles."

They erupted into exclamations of recognition, and one of them flashed me a thumbs-up. "Nice drive-by reference," he said.

Hey, I thought to myself. I *know* something. I'm one of the literature experts around here. If you're having a literary emergency of any sort, call Dr. Lang; he knows what the hell he's talking about.

First Day of Teaching (continued). A dozen bodies slouch at desks scattered around the classroom, more than a teacher would usually see seven minutes before the start of an 8:30 class. But these are freshmen, and this is their first day of school, too. I remind myself of what the experts always say when they talk about confronting wild animals: they are just as scared of you as you are of them.

I hope so.

The three years I spent doing research on college-level teaching and advising other people on how to teach have filled my head with many pedagogical ideals. Two of them were operating on me as I walked to class this morning:

1. If you want to establish rapport with students and create a good climate for discussion, arrive in class at least five minutes early and try to engage them in casual conversation.

2. The first day of class is the most important day of the semester. It sets the tone for the semester and should offer students a taste of what they will be experiencing throughout the course. Do not just walk in, read the syllabus, and let them go early. Engage them. Get them excited about starting the semester.

But as I look around me now, the idea of engaging these students in casual conversation seems laughable. Slumped in their chairs, either apathetic or trying to look that way, most of them aren't even making eye contact with me. They are looking at their books or doodling on an open notebook page or staring straight ahead, glassy-eyed. Believe me, I feel like telling them, I don't want to be here any more than you do. Let's all just go home. I won't tell if you won't.

I spend a good three minutes straightening papers on my desk, arranging and rearranging the handouts, and then I do what I always do when I'm nervous and have a few minutes to kill: I go to the bathroom. When I return, I see that a few new bodies have arrived. That's all they are to me at the moment, and will be for the next week or two: indistinguishable bodies in casual summer clothes, baseball hats and tennis shoes or tight t shirts and jeans shorts.

I don't wear a watch. The clock on the wall tells me it's 4:30 in the afternoon, but it's got to be 8:30 by now. I consult my lesson plan one last time, come out from behind the desk, and look out at fifteen faces. I'm trying very hard to imagine that they are just as scared as I am. And then, in the instant before I open my mouth, the thought of another scared student flashes across my mind.

First Days of a New Life. Tomorrow Katie will be starting kindergarten.

Since I don't teach on Wednesdays and Anne doesn't have to be at work until nine, we have made plans to walk Katie down to school together and see her off on her first day. We are both a little emotional about it, me especially. Anne, who has taught elementary school for almost a decade now, is used to seeing small children on their first day of school. But I choke up at the thought of my little four-year-old baby in a kindergarten classroom. It just doesn't seem possible that I could have a child old enough to be in school.

The first day in our new home had almost equaled the trauma I will feel on Katie's first day of school. We had spent three days driving from Chicago to Massachusetts, with one-night stopovers at my parents' home in Cleveland and a hotel in Pennsylvania. With a four-year-old and a two-year-old on board, we were not prepared to subject our nerves to more than six hours in the car per day.

During our three years in our house in Chicago we had accumulated enough stuff to require a professional moving company. We had so much stuff, in fact, that when the movers had filled their truck with our possessions, they weren't finished. So they had to call for a second truck, and we set out on the drive to Cleveland with furniture still scattered on our back lawn, the movers waiting for the second truck.

The afternoon we arrived in Worcester, we went directly to the lawyer's office and closed on the house we had purchased. We stayed in a hotel that night and the next morning met the moving van at our new house. We discovered that the second truck, which was carrying our bed, would not arrive for another two weeks. Later that day, as we explored the house with our daughters, we discovered that the previous owners had taken the washer and drier with them, not believing them to be "fixed" appliances. And a few days later we discovered that the people who had bought our house in Chicago were threatening to sue us because of the infestation of mice they found when they knocked out some closet walls.

On top of all this, I have just begun battling a very active flare-up of my Crohn's disease, a chronic illness I was diagnosed with four years previously. I am bleeding along my intestinal tract and have a constant case of diarrhea. I am very tired, and I need to see a doctor and to get a prescription or two, but I am in that transitional state of still being on my old insurance but living in a new place, and besides: where am I going to find the time to take care of my health with the start of the semester just a couple of days off?

First Day of Class (continued). I have what I think is an innovative plan for the first day, and I stick to it despite my desire to throw copies of the syllabus at my students and run from the room sobbing tears of relief. I am going to engage them by introducing the course, asking them to read a short, controversial essay, and leading a brief discussion. Afterwards, in the warm glow that follows an exciting intellectual conversation, I will hand out the syllabus and whet their appetite for the course.

So I introduce the course, which takes four minutes less than the five minutes I had allotted in my lesson plan, then give them the essay. I pace, waiting for them to finish reading and give me a signal that they are ready to talk—fold their hands on the desk and look up at me expectantly, perhaps?

Most of them just keep staring at the article, even those who are obviously done reading. Finally I decide I can't postpone things any longer, however desperately I want to. The moment I begin this discussion will be the moment I could begin failing in my new job. Thus far I haven't done anything wrong. My teaching record in my first year on the tenure track is still perfect.

But I can't wait any longer; it's time to speak. The article they have read describes a court case in which someone sued a television station for airing a show about rape that inspired a copycat crime. I begin by asking for a show of hands: how many of you think the girl's lawsuit was valid?

Two people raise their hands, very tentatively, palms at ear level.

"How many of you think it isn't valid?"

Three people raise their hands.

I'm no math professor, but even I can tell that those numbers don't add up to fifteen.

"OK," I say, "so some of you are undecided. Can someone tell me why you think the suit is valid or invalid, or why you can't decide?"

Silence. Complete stillness. Complete, panic-inducing silence and stillness. I count to ten, forcing myself to wait for a hand to go up. Fourteen people are looking at their desks, but one is looking right at me, a barely perceptible smile on his face. He is distinguishable to me only because of the Red Sox baseball hat that he will wear every day for the entire semester. He has cropped brown hair and wears shorts and a t-shirt—a look that doesn't do much to set him apart from his peers. His expression indicates either that he wants me to call on him or that he is enjoying watching me fall on my face.

I point to him. "What's your name, and what do you think?"

He wanted to be called on. His name is Ben. He launches into an answer that touches on a few of the more superficial arguments in the case. But that's OK. At least he spoke. I can help move him to the next level. That's my job, after all.

"OK, that's great," I say. "Anyone else?"

Of course not. I point to a few more people, but their answers are lackluster. They are doing their best not to commit to either side. I suspect they think I have a right answer in mind, and they don't want to be the fool who argues for the wrong side.

After ten minutes of this, I give up. I'll start fresh on Thursday. I hand out the syllabus, review the course policies, and we are out of there by 9:10, thirty-five minutes shy of the official end of class.

First Days of Meetings. In the two weeks before classes are scheduled to start, I have three full days of meetings to attend.

The first of these is the college's New Faculty Orientation, which takes place on Thursday, August 17, a week and a half before classes are scheduled to start. It lasts a full day, with a continental breakfast and lunch on the college. There are more than a dozen of us new faculty seated around a squared-up line of tables—later I will learn that not all of us are tenure track, and that some of the participants have been adjuncts at the college for a year or two already—along with another dozen members of the college staff or administration.

In the morning we are introduced to the members of the senior administration, all of whom have different things to tell us about the college, about its students, and about how we should teach them. A few details stand out in my mind.

The president of the college tells us that Assumption College students need quizzes. Give quizzes as often as possible, he warns us, or students will not stay on top of the reading. I silently dismiss this advice. *My* students won't need quizzes to stay on top of the reading. They will be so inspired by my teaching that they will be reading ahead.

(Prophetic aside: I'll be giving quizzes, of a sort, by the second semester.)

The acting dean of the college, who normally serves as the chair of the education department, offers advice on teaching, both theoretical and practical. On the practical side, she warns us, half-jokingly, that the registrar will get annoyed if we don't return the pencils with the evaluation forms the students fill out at the end of the semester.

Most of what they tell us is aimed at filling in the portrait of the typical Assumption student. We get some basic demographic facts: the students are mostly white, mostly Catholic, and mostly from New England. A third of them are first-generation college students. Reading between the lines, I gather that these are students who either did not have the academic record for, or were apprehensive about the size of, larger Catholic schools like Boston College or Providence College. These demographic figures help a bit. But right up to lunchtime we are still asking questions about the students. The more we talk about it, the more elusive the concept of the typical Assumption student seems to be.

We are told, for example, that the typical Assumption student is extremely courteous. She will often e-mail or telephone your office if she knows she will be missing class. The typical Assumption student is extremely intelligent, as smart as the best students we encountered at our Ph.D. institutions. But these comments seem to be at odds with the advice we are getting about giving quizzes, making sure that the students stay on top of the work, contacting our advisees regularly, letting the dean of studies know if we encounter students who are having trouble. For such nice, smart students, they sure seem to have a lot of problems.

Most of the afternoon is devoted to analyzing the source of many of those problems: alcohol. The alcohol and drug counselor and the residential life officer spend what seems to me a disproportionate amount of time talking about how much the students drink and how careful we must be not to make light of student alcohol use, how we must avoid parties or places where students are drinking and report any potential problem situations or students.

Afterwards, a new faculty member from the sciences raises his hand. "So if we see a student at a bar drinking, or see a student walking across campus who looks inebriated, do we have to report him?"

Several people step in to answer this one, all in the negative. Such a question never would have occurred to me, but once he voices it, I can understand why. He's feeling what we're all feeling: he's the new guy, he doesn't know the rules, and he wants to impress everyone with his desire to learn them and get it right.

The orientation is about as interesting and helpful as orientations ever are. It would be great if they held it two months into the semester, when I had the space in my brain to absorb the information—and the experience with students and the campus that would allow me to make practical use of it. A week before the semester begins, though, everything pretty much washes into one ear and out the other.

On Tuesday and Wednesday of the following week, I attend a two-day departmental retreat to revamp our department's two service courses (Freshman Composition and Introduction to Literature), to identify their specific educational objectives, and to define how we know when students have met those objectives. We also work on preparing the documents we will need for the accreditation process the college will soon be undergoing. The college must prepare reams of documents for the visitors from the accrediting organization, and each department and office must contribute its share of paper marked all up with printer ink.

These two days of meetings are long, but they are somewhat interesting, despite the endless debates about such questions as whether we want our students to "analyze" or to "interpret" literature. The discussions are cordial. Though we argue, we are arguing on what I take to be good terms. No one is insulting or dismissive, and I feel that we are willingly engaged in a shared enterprise. I leave the meetings—despite a lingering tinge of resentment about the hours they have stolen from my course preparation time—energized and excited to be joining the department and beginning my career on the tenure track.

First Day of Class (continued). Back in my office, I sit and try to get control of myself. OK, so it didn't go as well as I expected; it still wasn't a complete disaster. My fly was closed, I didn't trip over the cord for the overhead projector as I walked around the room, and nobody complained or insulted me. Things could have been worse.

I send an e-mail to a former colleague at Northwestern. "It has been quite some time since I taught an 8:30 class of freshmen who were taking a required course," I write, "so in retrospect I think I needed to do a little bit more to capture their attention." (It has actually been eight years since I taught one of those classes, in the first year of my M.A. program at St. Louis University, and I have obviously repressed my memories of those early-morning sessions.)

I spend the next hour reviewing my lesson plan for the 11:30 class and thinking about adjustments I might make in the 2:30 section of composition, where I have a chance to improve my morning lesson plan.

At 11:20 I trudge back over to Kennedy, to a larger classroom on the second floor. I have sixteen students enrolled in Contemporary British Fiction, an upper-level seminar in my area of expertise. This is the course I have been trained to teach. Moreover, these are upperclassmen, and many of them are English majors, so I have much higher expectations for this course than for composition.

I have the same lesson plan drawn up for this class as for composition: begin with an activity, then move into the standard stuff once I have caught their attention. But since that didn't work too well in the morning course, I decide to flip-flop the order: begin with the standard stuff and finish with the activity.

My written lesson plan instructs me to begin by introducing myself— telling them where I come from, what I studied, what I am interested in.

But looking at those sixteen blank faces, I just can't bring myself to do it. I go directly into talking about the course.

(This will happen frequently during my first year or two of teaching. Planning my lessons the afternoon or evening before class, I will write notes or devise interactive activities that strike me as innovative, exercises that will push beyond the boundaries of ordinary college courses. But then, standing at the front of the classroom, anxious about trying out the new lesson or technique, I will often skip those notes, abandon those activities, and resort to a back-up lesson plan of talking or conducting a traditional discussion. Usually this will mess up my timing, and class will end early, since I never give quite as much thought to my back-up lesson plans as I do to the real ones.)

Having skipped the personal introduction and described the course, I read over the syllabus with the students. I hate doing this—they can read, after all—but it's one of those legalistic tactics I have learned to use. At the end of the semester, when the student who has missed ten classes or plagiarized a paper doesn't understand why he failed, I can remind him that I read the attendance and plagiarism policies to him back in September.

After the syllabus reading, I conduct an exercise designed to help the students begin to think about differences between British and American fiction, in a world in which most English-speaking societies have free markets, McDonalds, television, and rock music. I ask them to write down in their notebooks a list of things they think of when they think of England today. They do that for a few minutes, and then I ask for people to volunteer their answers and help me make a list on the board.

"Princess Diana," responds a young woman with long blond hair and a raspy, cigarette-inflected voice who walked into class three minutes late.

"Good," I say, writing her answer on the board. "What else?"

They are much more chatty than my 8:30 freshmen, and it goes well. Many of the things they mention can be tied into one of the themes we will encounter throughout the semester, and I group their impressions into categories that correspond to those themes. Princess Diana, along with all other comments about royalty, goes under the category of "Class and

Economics," a major theme in British fiction. I feel that we are actually doing something substantive, a feeling reaffirmed by the sight of them scribbling away in their notebooks as I speak. I feel too a powerful surge of adrenaline as I stand at the front of the classroom, pointing at waving hands and transcribing my students' ideas onto the board. This is what I am here for; this is what I have been waiting for.

We still end a little early, but I feel redeemed from my 8:30.

I can do this.

Firsts. Like almost every event that has been long built up in the imagination, my first day of teaching was a little anticlimactic. Once I made it past the final moment of terror, at 8:29 A.M., and had concluded that first class, I could begin to foresee the grooves in which the semester would proceed—grooves that extended into the future from the courses I had taught as a graduate student and then as a lecturer at Northwestern. I don't suppose anyone begins a tenure-track job these days without having taught a few classes as a graduate student or an adjunct. Students are very different from institution to institution, obviously—and negotiating those differences can present a serious challenge, as I will learn—but the basic elements of the business remain the same.

The anticlimactic nature of that first day stemmed too, I think, from the fact that I had spent the month after my arrival being overwhelmed by first encounters: new house, new neighbors, new colleagues, new expectations, new schools and sitters for my children, new church, new license plates, new cable company, new yard to mow. That first day in the classroom, so long anticipated, got a little swamped by all those other firsts. And I wasn't the only one in the house having first days, either: my wife and older daughter had their first days of school, my younger daughter had her first day with a new daycare sitter. Their first days distracted me from constant apprehension about my first day in the classroom; near-constant was all I could manage.

One thing I did before my first day in the classroom that proved mildly helpful in dispelling my opening-day jitters was to spend plenty of time on campus beforehand and visit the classrooms in which I would be teaching. A professor speaking at a function at the Searle Center once said that before every class he taught, he walked once entirely around the classroom, making the space his own. I did the same thing here, stepping into each corner of the classroom, sitting at the desk, writing something on the board. When I arrived in those three different classrooms on that first Tuesday, the one familiar element of the experience was the space, and that familiarity helped.

As for the pedagogical side of that first day in front of the classroom, well . . . I almost hate to say this, but it would have been better to aim low. In my fourth year now, I do plan full and exciting lessons for the first days of my classes, and I carry through with my plans. I often wish more faculty would join me in doing so, since not all students would then expect the first day of every one of their classes to be a blow-off. But I think it was a mistake to aim so high on my first day in a new institution, facing new students, in a new classroom.

For that *very* first day, of my *very* first semester—if I had to do it again?

I would get in there, read them the syllabus, take questions, and let them go early.

First Day of Class (concluded). After the fiction class, I sit at my computer for a while, eating the sandwich and banana I packed for lunch and checking e-mail. I make sure to finish my lunch before my scheduled office hour at 1:30; I don't want to greet students with a mouthful of turkey, cheese, and white bread.

Not to worry—no visitors during today's office hour, just as there were none yesterday. Yesterday was the first official day of the semester, a day for students to register and make last-minute changes to their schedules, so I held my regular office hours even though classes hadn't yet met.

My afternoon composition class is in a classroom two floors below my office. It has a large support column running from floor to ceiling in the center of the room, a feature that will disconcert me throughout the semester. If the desks are arranged in traditional rows, someone is always sitting behind that beam, no matter where I stand. It's as if I had bought tickets for the cheap seats behind a pole at the baseball game; some part of my view is always obstructed.

The class runs pretty much like the morning one, with a slightly more animated and extended conversation. Students in the 2:30 class aren't still groggy from having just woken up; they are simply a bit drowsy from missing their afternoon naps. I will eventually figure out that the 11:30 is the only class in which my students aren't missing potential sleep time. They're missing their lunch, but at least they're awake.

I had contemplated making major adjustments to the lesson plan for the afternoon but decided against it, because I wanted the classes to have the same experience on the first day. I can foresee already that having the same class twice in one day will pose a continuous dilemma. On the one hand, it gives me the opportunity to make adjustments if things go badly in the first section. On the other hand, if I adjust too much, then I may throw the classes out of sync, raising the dreadful specter of having to prepare two different lesson plans for the same class as the semester progresses.

After class I hang around my office for a bit—still no visitors—my body still pumping with adrenaline from the emotional swings of my first day. I linger in the hallway talking with my next-door office neighbor, Mark, who was also newly hired this year.

Mark teaches on a Monday-Wednesday-Friday schedule this semester and has four courses. (We teach a three-four load, meaning that we have three courses in one semester and four in the other.) He asks me how my day went, and I try to put as positive a face on it as I can. I certainly don't want him to know that I bombed my morning class.

I ask him about his plans for tomorrow. He tells me, with obvious enthusiasm, about his plans for Introduction to Journalism. He is taking it one step further than I did. He's not handing out the syllabus at all. Instead, he plans to give the students their first assignment. They will have ten minutes to prepare questions, then they will interview him about the course and write a story about it for the next class, when they will get the syllabus and the usual information about the course.

It sounds great to me, and I hope it goes well. At this particular moment, though, fresh off my failures, I am a little fearful for him.

"What about your other classes?" I ask.

"I'm just giving them the syllabus and letting them go early."

Teaching

Having survived my first day, I have the arrogance to presume that I have learned my lesson and that I am past the danger of falling flat on my face. Mistake.

Thursday, September 7, 2000, 8:30 A.M. Our fourth class together.

For today's class I assigned a story by James Joyce called "The Encounter." The narrator, a young Irish boy, describes how he was inspired by pulp novels about the American West to take a day off from school and embark upon an adventure. The adventure becomes a sordid and depressing affair that concludes with a disturbing encounter with a vaguely predatory old man. My plan is to divide the students into groups—the first time I have tried this with this class—and have them answer some questions about what the story suggests about the relationship between art and life.

I arrange the groups so that they are mixed with respect to skill level, based on a diagnostic essay assignment I had administered on the second day of class to test their initial writing skills. I make sure that each group has one student who performed well on the assignment and one who did not. According to an article I had read at the Searle Center, this is the best way to ensure good learning in group activities: make the groups as heterogenous as possible, especially with respect to skill level. Poor students benefit from the tutoring of their stronger peers; the good students learn the material better as a result of having taught it to others.

Each group gets a worksheet that asks them to write their responses to three simple questions:

What happens in the story?

Why does it happen?

How would you finish this sentence: The encounter teaches the boy . . . ?

These seem like such softball questions that I am almost ashamed to ask them. It seems glaringly self-evident that the encounter teaches the boy that real life often turns out to be not as glamorous as the life we see depicted in comics, books, or films.

I know from experience that the first few moments of group work can be the most awkward ones. No student wants to be the first to break the silence in the classroom, especially with the teacher hovering around. So I use my standard technique for getting them past that awkward moment: once I have handed out the worksheets and told them to get started, I step out of the room for a drink of water and hang out in the hallway for a couple of minutes. By the time I get back, discussions are usually under way.

But today I come back to a still-silent room. No one looks at me. They are all looking at the book, or at their still-blank handout sheets.

"What's the matter?" I ask.

Ben looks up at me questioningly from beneath his Red Sox hat, that same small smile on his face. He is in a group with Nick and Linda, both students who had turned in weaker performances on the diagnostic essay.

"We don't really understand what we're supposed to be doing," he says.

"OK," I respond, a little taken aback. "What part of it don't you understand?"

"Well, do you want us to just tell you what the story was about?"

"I want you just to note down the main developments in the plot, the ones that lead up to the encounter at the end. You can just put them in a list of phrases on your worksheet."

"Oh," he says. He still seems uncertain. "OK."

"Really? Are you sure you understand? Does everyone else understand?"

I look around the room. Everyone is just staring at me. I have a momentary flash of angry frustration. I can understand them not wanting to participate in a discussion about literature at 8:30 in the morning, but can't they at least nod their heads in response to a direct question?

"Listen," I say. "Just take five minutes and outline the plot, and we'll talk about the other two questions together as a class."

And just like that, my lesson plan has fallen apart—or, more accurately, I have dismantled it. The plot summaries they write are all over the place, the discussion that follows falters and quickly dries up, and I pack up my books at the end of the hour with the faintest sense of desperate foreboding. If I don't turn this thing around within the next week or two, this could be a long semester. And the worst part of that failure would be that I came into the semester with such high hopes, such grand expectations, and such confidence.

Flush with the knowledge gained during my three years studying college-level teaching at the Searle Center, I planned an innovative and experimental Freshman Composition course. The entire semester will focus on a single topic: the relationship between art—broadly defined, including books, music, films, even television commercials—and ethics. We will study how television violence affects children; we will read works in which characters talk about the influence of books and art on their behavior; we will listen to controversial rock music and consider how it inspires certain emotions or actions. Students will write papers describing how works of art have influenced them, will analyze rock songs and films, and will research the psychological and philosophical literature on this issue. The centerpiece of the course will be a case study in which students will read *Huckleberry Finn*, as well as a series of arguments about whether it is a racist novel, and submit a report to a fictional high school principal arguing for or against keeping the novel as part of a required curriculum.

The idea for this course had come from my work at the center, where we spent a lot of time and energy studying, and persuading others to experiment with, courses in which students were confronted with real-life scenarios or problems and had to use knowledge learned in the course in order to negotiate that scenario. I had read about and even observed fascinating courses in which students put historical figures on trial, built functional robots, or filed reports to government officials about hypothetical scenarios devised by the professor.

So I designed my composition course according to this model. Of course, I am also responsible for teaching my students how to write academic essays—a responsibility that limits the real-world scenarios I might use to construct the course. (Somehow this just doesn't seem plausible: "The client needs a five-hundred-word analysis of a James Joyce story, and your boss wants it on his desk by noon tomorrow!") But I think I have put together something worthwhile, something that will engage students in real-life questions.

In fact, I have such confidence in the value of this course design that I have approached a friend at a major educational publisher, a former graduate school colleague, about putting together a composition text based on this topic. I have approached a second publisher as well, with an informal e-mail query to the acquisitions editor. Both of them are interested in seeing a proposal, so I am hoping to use the course as a way to identify appealing readings, construct sample assignments, refine the scope of the inquiry, and be well under way with a book project that would certainly count towards tenure at a teaching-focused college like mine.

I know: planning a project like this in my first semester sounds overly ambitious. But I really didn't imagine that I would have to write all that much to make progress on such a project. Constructing assignments and selecting readings was all work I would be doing for the course anyway. To make progress on the book project, I had only to write down what worked and what didn't.

But I was so interested in the design of this particular course that it never occurred to me that it might not work—that students would have no interest in the topic I had chosen. And now here we are, two weeks into the semester, and not a single student has shown one iota of interest, I can't get anyone to speak, and they all seem unwilling or unable to complete even the simplest assignment.

Composition is not the only realm in which I am crashing and burning. That first day in Contemporary British Fiction, which went as well as I could have hoped, has been followed by a series of discussions that go primarily like this:

I pose a question.
A student responds.

I ask a follow-up question.
A different student responds.
I ask for any other thoughts on the same question.
No one responds.
I ask a new question.
Another student responds.

Proceeding according to this pattern, and considering that it takes, say, two minutes for me to formulate a question and for a student to answer it, I will need to prepare thirty-five different questions per day if I want to teach that class by means of discussion. Maybe forty, to allow for the occasional question that elicits no response at all.

Equally troubling is the fact that a handful of students respond to the questions very regularly, while a much larger group of them simply sit and listen. Teri, the raspy-voiced woman who volunteered the first response on the first day, regularly contributes. She is also self-aware, which I like. Sometimes she glances around pointedly before she raises her hand, as if to assure me that she does not want to dominate the conversation. Her friend Charlotte contributes as well. They come in together every day, usually just as I am starting class. Charlotte—with shoulder-length brown hair, a soft voice, and a friendly, open disposition—offers thoughtful responses that show me she has done the reading. I am happy to have both of them in class, even if I would sometimes like to hear from other students.

The student from whom I most want to hear is a reluctant contributor. I have received their first short papers, written in response to the first novel they read. I was happy with the quality of their written work. These upperclassmen were far more skilled in writing and analysis than the level of their contributions in class would indicate. But Margaret's paper came out of nowhere. It was as intelligent and insightful as any student paper I have ever read. In truth, I would have been happy to put my name on that paper. But Margaret—pale skin, glasses, curly red hair, a silver cross on a necklace—is obviously a quiet student, and I can get her to respond only when I specifically invite her into the discussion.

I find myself relying more frequently than I would like on the strategy of "cold-calling": identifying specific people and inviting them into the conversation. I have read arguments both for and against this practice. My former director at the Searle Center, Ken Bain, ultimately convinced me that cold-calling is fine, as long as you think of it as inviting someone to an intellectual feast rather than challenging him to a duel. So I have been issuing quite a few invitations in this class, trying to make sure everyone's voice gets heard in the first couple of weeks. The longer they sit without speaking, I know from experience, the less likely it is that they will ever speak. So I invite a few new people into the conversation each class. It *has* had an effect on a few of them. A student I called on at the beginning of the third class participated regularly for the rest of that class and the next one. But the effect hasn't exactly snowballed into an avalanche of animated debates.

I'm beginning to wonder: How much time do I have, in all three of my classes, until I have to chalk this up as a lost semester?

I decide to turn to my colleagues for help.

I know they face the same challenges I am facing. During my on-campus interview for the job, I had a forty-five-minute session with the entire department. During that part of the interview, someone told me that Assumption students can be reluctant to speak up in class and asked me how I would encourage participation in a silent classroom. I gave a few stock answers, but at the time I dismissed the premise of the question. My reading of the literature on teaching and learning had taught me that faculty at just about every college in the country believe that their students are notoriously silent. It's one of those myths that exist at all colleges, like stories about how the library was built without taking into account the weight of the books, and now (gasp!) it's sinking a few inches every year.

After my first two weeks, though, I am starting to wonder. In the past my greatest strength as a teacher has been my ability to provoke class debates and discussions. I never had a shortage of students willing to jump into the discussion and often had to choose between many hands desperately waving for my attention.

Three doors down from me is another junior professor, who is in his third year at Assumption. Ed is in his early forties, short, stocky, white-haired, reserved but pleasant. Originally from New England, he came here with his wife, also an academic, from a small college in Alabama. He teaches Shakespeare, runs the English Club, and started a local chapter of Sigma Tau Delta, the English honor society. Students are constantly streaming into and out of his office, and I have heard from other faculty that his classes are usually full. I also know from overheard hallway conversations that he likes baseball and beer—two of my favorite things—so I would like to befriend him.

One afternoon as I am coming back from the department office with my mail, I see him through his open office door, sitting at his desk. I decide to see if I can learn his secrets. I knock, and he beckons me in, motioning me to sit in the chair he keeps for students. His office, like mine—and like all the faculty offices in our building—is a former dorm room. It has built-in wardrobes on either side of the door and a large window opposite the door, looking into the woods behind the building. Against the side walls, towards the window, are recessed niches where the students once had their beds.

Ed's office is shadowed and cozy, with throw rugs on the floor and bookshelves lining one entire wall. Conference posters, postcard images of Shakespeare, and pictures of students cover the walls and the door. I have kept my office minimally decorated to this point, with just two bookshelves, two file cabinets, my desk, a small table, and no pictures or posters. I can see why students feel comfortable in Ed's office, which reminds me of someone's den. Mine looks like a doctor's examining room. I make a mental note to try to cozy up my office.

I tell him what's on my mind.

"So I guess what I want to know," I finish, "is what you do in the classroom. How do you get them to speak up?"

"It's tough," he says with a shrug, raising his eyebrows. "They don't want to talk."

"So what do you do?"

"I ask questions. I ask them questions and expect them to answer."

"What if no one responds?"

"I ask the question again, or ask a different one."

His answers are terse, but they are delivered in a sympathetic way that seems to invite further conversation. This is one of the qualities, I will learn throughout the year, that draws students to his office.

However, the more we talk, the more I realize that Ed has no answers for me. In fact, the more I press him about his specific teaching methods, the more I sense that he teaches in a more traditional style than I do: he lectures and then asks discussion questions. Judging from his popularity with students and the respect our colleagues have for him, he clearly knows how to make this teaching style work. But I don't feel comfortable with that style—I prefer a more varied slate of interactive exercises—so I thank Ed for his perspective and head back to my office in about the same boat I left in.

As September moves along and I engage more of my colleagues in conversations about teaching, seeking advice from both senior and junior faculty, I develop a growing suspicion that many other teachers here—far more than I would have dreamed—use the traditional method of lectures peppered with occasional questions.

Given the small size of the college and of the classes, I had imagined, before I arrived, that a school like this—one that evaluates its faculty primarily on their teaching skills—would be a hotbed of innovative teaching methods. I understood why so many faculty at Northwestern relied on the lecture method, given the size of the classes. Here it doesn't make much sense to me.

The classroom I teach in at 8:3o is connected by a door to another classroom, and when my class is silent—either when my discussions are failing miserably or when the students are writing or reviewing each other's work—I can hear the professor next door teaching one of the college's general-education courses. She has a distinctive high-pitched voice that would drive me crazy if I had to listen to it for very long. And as far as I can tell, throughout my first month of teaching—and this will continue throughout the entire semester—*she never shuts up.*

One day, curious about whether the size of the class is dictating this constant lecturing, I step out of my classroom while my students are doing their writing exercise and peer through the open door of her classroom. She is at the podium, lecturing away. Scattered among the thirty or so desks are fourteen students, all of them apparently comatose with boredom.

If I were to approach her after class and ask why she feels it necessary to lecture to fourteen students, I am sure she would say that she has an obligation to "cover" the material. My time at the Searle Center has given me a different perspective. Material needs to be covered, but teaching exclusively by lecture—or exclusively by any method—doesn't strike me as the right solution. If you need material covered, have the students read it. Lecture about it some, to synthesize and supplement, but also spend time listening to the students—on paper or in class—to ensure that they are processing what you are "covering."

Still, despite my convictions in this area, I'm tempted, two weeks into the semester, to give in and just start lecturing. It may require me to write reams of new class notes, but at least I wouldn't have to deal with the uncertainties and anxiety of attempting to run an interactive classroom. If you misspeak or forget a chunk of your lecture, you can just bluster ahead and move on to new material. But if no one wants to participate in your interactive activity, you're screwed. Class is over.

The one thing that stops me from falling into lecture mode is that I am a *terrible* lecturer. For reasons that have never been clear to me, I cannot lecture effectively about literature. A lecture from me about postwar British fiction could put to sleep a coffeehouse full of amphetamine addicts.

So I have no choice but to soldier on and keep trying to engage students in the ways I am comfortable with, even when they aren't working. I find some solace in the knowledge that I have one colleague who practices an even more interactive teaching style than I: Mark, my next-door neighbor.

Mark is a former journalist who spent a decade in Alabama writing for newspapers before returning to graduate school to earn his Ph.D. in fiction writing. These days he mostly writes pieces in the same genre as my *Chronicle* columns: the personal essay or creative nonfiction. Mark is a huge man: six-five, at least 275 pounds, with shaggy graying hair and beard. He is one of the friendliest people I have ever met, with a gentle Southern affability, and he and his dog have quickly become a fixture around campus and in the hallways and offices of our building. His body, his look, his persona, all seem perfect for the role of the gregarious and lovable author, downing Scotches as a crowd of admirers hangs onto every word of his latest yarn.

Mark was hired to teach writing courses and has a full load of them. From our frequent hallway conversations I can tell that he teaches an almost exclusively student-centered class. He lays out the basic principles and then acts as a coach as the students critique each other's application of those principles in their work. He has been doing group work and interactive exercises right from the start, and has encountered some of the same bumps I have. But he shows no signs of changing his teaching style, and no signs of flagging in his enthusiasm. He is familiar with much of the literature on teaching and writing that I have read, and he seems confident that it will eventually start to have an effect. I am heartened enough by that to keep at it myself.

It's music that finally begins to draw them out of their shells.

In the British fiction course we are reading *A Clockwork Orange,* by Anthony Burgess, a horrifying novel set in the London of the not-too-distant future, narrated by a fifteen-year-old boy who leads a gang of teenagers on sprees of vandalism, rape, and terrorization every evening after dark. This narrator, Alex, has only one seemingly redeeming quality: he is an aficionado of classical music, especially Beethoven. At one point in the narrative, though, he explains that listening to Beethoven's music, especially the Fifth and Ninth Symphonies, helps put him in the mood for his violent nighttime excursions. By giving this awful character a love for classical music, and having him tell us that it inspires him to violence, Burgess makes the point that we all react to art differently. Art can't really be said to teach us anything, or influence us to do anything specific, or make us better people, as many philosophers, writers, and literary theorists have argued.

I decide to conduct an experiment to see whether this critique holds true in the classroom. I bring in my CD player and a copy of Beethoven's Ninth. As we listen to the fourth movement of the symphony, the "Ode to Joy," I tell the students to write down in their notebooks whatever emotions it inspires in them. Afterwards, we will compare notes and see whether Burgess is right—that the same piece of music can inspire a host of differing emotions and ideas.

Of course it does, and the range of emotions the students note down is surprisingly wide—from feelings of serenity and piety to ones of violent energy, from sadness to joy, from triumph to depression. For the first time, it feels as if this class and I have worked together to discover something worth knowing. Although I essentially forced everyone to participate, their comments came willingly, and they seemed interested in hearing the responses of their peers.

One good class—sometimes that's all it takes in this business to redeem a dozen failures. Teaching, in this respect, reminds me of golf. Eighteen miserable holes of golf can be redeemed by that one perfect drive, or that approach shot that nestles to within a few inches of the pin. So a month's worth of dying up in front of the blackboard is washed away by the surge of elation over the impassioned debate you've been waiting for all semester.

Emboldened by my success with music in the fiction class, I try a parallel experiment in composition. As it happens, we are in the unit of the course in which the students are writing an analysis of a rock song of their choosing. They have to analyze and interpret the lyrics and then explain how the musical elements of the song support their interpretation. So the following week I cart my CD player into the classroom, along with a Dave Matthews Band CD and an overhead with the lyrics to "Ants Marching," one of the countless rock songs that lament the conformity imposed on us by modern urban life. I put the overhead up, play the song, and ask the students to help me interpret the lyrics.

We go through the song line by line, and they are quite good at it. The energy level in the room is higher than usual, and although the participation does not skyrocket to unparalleled heights, they are clearly interested. I can read in their comments and their glances at one another that they are surprised to learn that a professor has even heard of Dave Matthews, much less that he owns one of his CDs. They probably think about me the way my daughter thinks about her kindergarten teacher. We saw her teacher out on a weekend day, and Katie was shocked to discover that she didn't live at school. My students no doubt think I live in my office and spend all my time reading great literature and thinking about my classes.

After we have discussed the Matthews song, I play a different song and ask them to interpret it on their own, in groups. This time the groups are clear on the task, and they work at it. Again, it feels as though we are doing something substantial, something that has engaged them and is helping to develop their thinking skills.

It feels, in other words, as though I am finally starting to do my job.

In the weeks that follow these successful classes, I am tempted to just keep bringing music into every class—to replicate this one technique that worked so well. But a few days' reflection on what made this technique successful—the underlying pedagogical principles—convinces me that such specific replication is not necessary.

"Pedagogical principles" makes it sound as if I had thought very deliberately about this technique and applied it systematically to achieve the result that came about. This is not the case. In those first four or five weeks of teaching, I was trying anything and everything I could think of. I threw it all against the wall, hoping something would eventually stick. It was only after the music technique stuck that I went back and figured out what made it work and began to think about how I could apply it in other forms.

The exercise with Beethoven helped me see that I needed to build a foundation for my classroom discussions, one based on what I have come to think of as preliminary fact-finding exercises. At Northwestern I could have walked into a classroom full of students who had read *A Clockwork Orange* and asked them the question that most interested me about the book: Does the author suggest that the narrator is evil because of his environment—which includes the classical music he listens to—or because of some natural, inherent inclination? The debate would have taken off from there. But with my Assumption students—who are all intellectually capable but need a bit of nudging to commit themselves to a discussion or an assignment—I have to step back from the big questions and lay the facts out first.

To get to the big question that interests me about the narrator and his environment, I do some preliminary exercises in the following class. I ask them, first, to write down in their notebooks the characteristics of the narrator that stand out. Then I ask them to do the same for his environment. We make two lists on the board, one about the narrator and one about his environment. Then, once we have done this work, I point to our collected data and ask them whether they can identify specific elements

34

of the narrator's environment and argue for or against the idea that his environment determines his behavior.

By the end of September I am consistently adding preliminary fact-finding missions to my lesson plans, and the participation levels ratchet up significantly. The students apparently find it easier, and less nerve-wracking, to volunteer concrete information than to jump into a debate. The participation levels, once we move into the debate, are still not where I want them to be, but they are improving noticeably.

The one drawback to all this tinkering with my customary lesson plan style is that it has thrown off my ability to time the lessons accurately. Most days the discussion or debate peters out ten to fifteen minutes short of the allotted seventy-five minutes of class time. I feel guilty about this and sometimes try to fill up these last minutes by talking about the next day's reading or summarizing again what we have concluded from today's class. Some days, though, I am as eager to get out of there as they are, and I just let them go early. Part of me wonders whether they are conscious of this and deliberately stop talking with ten or fifteen minutes left to go, hoping I will call it an early day.

The one class in which I can usually manage to keep the timing right is my final one of the day, the second composition class. This is in part because I have had the chance to practice my lesson plan on the morning class. It is also because I have made a much more immediate and personal connection with this class.

This difference has a lot to do with my attitude. When I walk into my 8:30 class, I don't want to be there. I'm not a morning person, for starters, and the beginning of that 8:30 class also means the beginning of my full day of teaching. I walk into the room knowing that I have three seventy-five-minute classes to teach and two different lesson plans—one for composition, one for British fiction—to keep straight in my head. So no matter how much I want to come in and start up casual conversation and joke around for a few minutes at the beginning of the 8:30 class, either I can't bring myself to do it at all, or I do it half-heartedly and it falls flat.

But when I walk into my 2:30 composition class, I have only seventy-five minutes to go until I am through for the day, and for the following day as well, when I only have office hours. I have nothing but the upcoming class on my mind, and I am relaxed going in, which means that I start conversations with the students and inject some humor into what I'm saying. And when I tell a joke here, unlike in my morning class, some of the students actually laugh.

I am learning personalities too, thanks in part to the first papers they wrote, about an experience of a work of art influencing their lives. Jamie wrote an excellent paper about seeing the band Live on *Saturday Night Live,* and being inspired by the lyrics and the energy of the group to form his own band. He plays the guitar, writes his own songs, and has the look of a musician: two-tone dyed hair and one of those shell necklaces that hug the neck. He came to my office with a draft of his second paper—something I have encouraged all my students to do, though only a handful have taken advantage of the offer. We talked about rock music and bands we both like. I asked him about his major plans, thinking I might nudge him towards English, but he has his mind set on biology and genetics. After we talk in my office he becomes a more frequent contributor in class.

Megan, a small woman who wears her blond hair pulled into a ponytail so tight that it seems to be stretching her face back, also wrote a terrific paper, about a painting that had been given to her by a family for whom she babysat throughout high school. She speaks up in class, and she too came to see me with a draft of her second paper, wanting feedback before she turned it in. After we finished discussing her paper, I asked her if she might be interested in babysitting our two daughters next semester, and she responded enthusiastically.

But the person who makes the firmest impression on me is Jack, a tall and gangly young man with short brown hair. Jack runs cross-country, and has the build for it. He has some nervous mannerisms, like rocking back and forth on his feet when he talks. He volunteers oddly self-deprecating stories about his personal life in front of the class, in a tone that keeps me guessing as to whether he is deliberately soliciting or blithely ignoring the snickers of his peers. I can't tell whether he is playing the class clown or is just a clown.

But I like him. He has stopped by my office a couple of times, without any specific issue to discuss. The first time this happened I kept waiting for him to bring up the paper that was due the following day.

"Uh, Jack," I finally said, during a lull in the conversation. "Did you want to talk about your paper at all?"

"Oh, no," he said, standing up to leave. "I haven't started that yet. I'm going to the library to work on it now."

"Oh. Well . . . good luck."

"See ya' round, Professor."

I dissected that encounter in my mind for a few minutes afterwards, wondering if I had missed some signal about what he wanted to discuss. Students at Northwestern *never* stopped by my office just to chat. Jack, I will learn as the year goes by, is the type of student who does. I do not do well with small talk and with making and maintaining casual acquaintances, but I am gratified that Jack feels comfortable enough with me to make these casual visits. And even though Megan and Jamie stopped by for a specific purpose, it still felt nice to have them in my office, and to work with them individually on their writing in a way that the classroom setting doesn't allow.

In the first week of October I decide to fall back on another recommendation we used to make to faculty at the Searle Center: administer midterm surveys to the students. I devise different surveys for each class, but each one asks three basic questions:

What has been least useful in helping you learn in this class?

What has been most useful in helping you learn in this class?

Do you have any comments or suggestions for me to help you learn more effectively in the class?

I pick a day, stop fifteen minutes early in each class, give out the surveys, and ask the students to fill them out anonymously and put them in an envelope on my desk on the way out. I don't expect an entirely accurate picture from these surveys, since I suspect at least some of the students will be reluctant to criticize me too harshly, fearing that this is some kind of teacher's trick to weed out malcontents. But I have done these surveys before at Northwestern, and they usually yield very useful information.

After each class, I take the surveys back to my office and immediately tear the envelope open, both wanting and not wanting to get the bad news. Most of the bad news comes from the 8:30 composition class, in which various students identify just about every activity I have tried as being "least helpful" to them in learning to write.

But even in that class, and especially in the British fiction class and the afternoon composition class, the comments are mostly positive. The majority of the students in British fiction offer some kind of unsolicited comment about how much they enjoy the interactive nature of the class. "Discussion," one student writes, "is so much better than lecture!"

While part of me is pleased with these responses, another part of me wants to tear my hair out in frustration. If all of them like discussion so much better than lecture, then why don't more of them participate in it?

What I really learn about from these surveys, aside from some specific modifications I need to make to each course, is the gap between my experience of the class and theirs. Discussions that seemed modestly successful to me obviously looked very different to them. On days when I announced at the beginning of class that we would be working in groups, I thought I picked up negative energy at the prospect; instead, on the surveys many of them identify the group work as one of their favorite parts of the class.

The surveys don't ultimately yield as much practical information as I would like, since so many of the comments cancel one another out. For every person who likes the workshops in which they read and critique their peers' papers, another person hates them. But at the very least, the surveys convince me that I have done the right thing by sticking to what I know and do best, and they give me hope that I may eventually learn—all over again—how to teach.

Writing

On the afternoon of August 31—a Thursday afternoon, after my last class for the week—I sent an e-mail to a friend from my former office at Northwestern:

> What I really can't get over is that I can sit here in my office and do my work and work at home and no one keeps watch over me or tells me what to do or notices how much time I'm logging etc. This is the kind of freedom I have been dreaming of over the past three years and it feels great ... And I actually have time to write now, and I can do it in the day when I want to rather than trying to punch stuff out at night when my brain is a little worn down.

At least a half-dozen e-mails I sent out in the early days of the semester described the great sense of freedom I felt at being liberated from the constraints of a nine-to-five work schedule.

I didn't realize, in those late days of August and early days of September, that this freedom would prove both a blessing and a curse. Nor did I realize that I was calculating my time demands based only on class preparations. Since my students had yet to turn in their first writing assignments, I had yet to figure in the amount of time I would need to dedicate to grading papers.

In September I worked with a friend, newly hired at a Catholic college in the Midwest, putting together a panel of papers on contemporary fiction for a conference in my field. He organized the panel; all I had to do was come up with a two-page abstract for my own paper and get it to him by the first of October.

Here is the e-mail I send him on October 6:

I got totally swamped with grading papers over the last two days and we are leaving in a half-hour for my sister's wedding in Cleveland. I have not done the abstract yet—my poor planning. We get back on Monday, and as soon as I can get the kids in bed I am going to work on the abstract. I will send it to you sometime that evening, although it might be late. I'm really sorry about this, John—I'm still having trouble figuring out how to budget my own time, now that I don't have to be in the office from nine to five every day! I'll talk to you soon.

So October comes, and reality sets in. The unstructured time that I initially saw as endlessly malleable, affording me the opportunity to write when I pleased, has all but disappeared. While I used to be able to count on having at least my evenings free to write, I no longer have any sacred writing time. Faced with a stack of forty composition papers to mark and return, I do nothing but grade in the time I can snatch away from helping to care for the children.

As each week of the semester passes, I find myself with less and less time to write. And I am teaching only three classes this semester. What will it be like next semester, when I am teaching four?

My initial plan for allowing myself time to write seemed modest enough.

My three classes were scheduled on Tuesday and Thursday, so obviously those days were out. Saturdays and Sundays were out, too. Those days are reserved for the children. I don't want to lock myself in the office or escape to the basement to write on the weekends while Anne watches the children; if nothing else, the guilt I would feel would keep me from getting anything done. So that left me Mondays, Wednesdays, and Fridays.

We are required to hold ten office hours per week—a number that seems high to me, given the sparse number of students who take advantage of the office hours. In my first six weeks on the tenure track I have spent maybe five of my sixty office hours talking with students.

I scheduled one office hour each on Tuesdays and Thursdays, then scheduled the remaining hours from ten to two on Mondays and Wednesdays. I left Fridays open. I imagined, then, that I would have time to write before ten on Mondays and Wednesdays and from eight to two on Fridays. My workdays have to end at two so that I can be home helping with the children when Katie is finished with kindergarten. Work usually starts up again, for at least another hour or two, at eight in the evening after the kids are in bed.

My Monday-morning writing session is the first to go. Although matters are improving, I am still struggling so much with my teaching that class preparation drains away much of my time—not to mention my powers of concentration. And since I can't spend my weekend preparing for class on Tuesday, I have to do it during my Monday writing time. While four office hours sounds like enough time to accomplish two class preps, somehow it never is.

Student visits don't come close to filling up my office hour time, but other little things usually do: reading and responding to e-mails from the college, the department, colleagues, and students; talking to colleagues who stop by, or whose offices I visit for counsel or commiseration; taking care of the many nuisance tasks that accompany a cross-country move, like finishing our business with lawyers, movers, and mortgage companies; trying to get someone to fix the malfunctioning VCRs in my classrooms; reading the materials that the chair sends around for the departmental meetings, which seem to take place every other week.

By the first week of October, my Wednesday-morning writing time is gone as well. I might have been able to sneak Wednesday's writing in if I only had to prepare for class and didn't have to grade papers. But with three classes, all writing intensive, another batch of papers always seems to be on its way in, so I increasingly find that I need to devote Wednesday mornings to grading the papers I haven't finished for return on Thursday.

That leaves Fridays. Friday writing time, at least so far, I am managing to keep more or less intact, although two family weekend trips to the beach have eaten away at it. I probably shouldn't even be setting aside Fridays as writing time. I could spend Friday doing my class preparations for the following week, and not be up until midnight doing it on Monday. But I find that I just can't focus on teaching on Fridays. My brain needs a different kind of work, and the prospect of those four open days before my next class deceives me into believing that I will find plenty of time for that later.

So now in October, I am writing on Fridays, and it looks as if that will be my only consistent writing day until the semester ends in early December.

This reduction in my writing time does not distress me as much as I would have expected it to, since I find, especially as the semester wears on, that I have nothing to write anyway.

Well, that's not entirely true. It might be more accurate to say that the intellectual energy required to teach two new classes, keep track of around fifty students, grade their work, and figure out how to be an assistant professor has left all my brain cells temporarily handling other calls. None of them are available to handle my writing requests at the moment, but if I hang on the line, my call will be taken in the order it was received.

I had established for myself some loosely defined—and, in retrospect, insanely ambitious—writing goals for my first semester on the tenure track:

1. Write two columns for the *Chronicle of Higher Education*, twelve hundred to fifteen hundred words each, on my first-semester experiences.

2. Revise into a separate essay, and prepare for submission to a journal, my dissertation chapter on the British novelist Ian McEwan. This will require no new research, just cutting and rewriting the introduction, conclusion, and transitions.

3. Draft an essay on Jeanette Winterson's novel *Oranges Are Not the Only Fruit*, which I can revise and prepare to submit over break. I will be teaching this novel in the fall, so I figure this will be a cakewalk. I will write the essay while teaching the book, and my research and teaching will coalesce nicely.

4. Write one or two additional short personal essays and identify possible publication outlets for them.

As the end of October approaches, the status of these four goals is as follows:

1. The *Chronicle* columns are the only writing goal I have any hope of meeting. I enjoy writing them, and the process makes my confusions and struggles more comprehensible to me.

Thus far I have written one column for the *Chronicle*. It was published on September 22. It reintroduced me to readers of the *Chronicle* and previewed the columns I would be writing this year. It also described the biggest change I have been grappling with in my life as an assistant professor: "The most prominent change in my working life has been the one that relates to my move from an administrative to a full-time faculty position: the management of my time."

(Looking back, from my fourth-year perspective, on the e-mails and columns I wrote during that first year, I am amazed that the management of my time was such a consistent source of surprise, frustration, and bafflement to me throughout the year.)

2. I am not the most ambitious scholar in the world, especially as my interest is slowly turning to more popular forms of writing. But I have been hired to teach twentieth-century British literature, and while publishing expectations here are low, they are not nonexistent. So I need to publish at least a few scholarly essays on post–World War II British fiction, my area of specialization.

This one should be easy. My dissertation chapter on Ian McEwan runs close to fifty pages, so I certainly have all the information I need. I should be able just to cut and rework the frame. So I pull the dissertation out of its box on a Thursday afternoon in early October and take it home with me. I sit down with it on Friday morning, cup of tea in hand, to reread the McEwan chapter and begin planning my revisions.

It has been over three years since I wrote those chapters, and I needed that time away. The very idea of looking at my dissertation within the first year of finishing it would have been enough to induce vomiting. In my second and third years after finishing it, I didn't go back to it because I was regularly writing essays about teaching for the Searle Center, and in my spare time I was working on two articles about a British novelist I had not treated in my dissertation, Kazuo Ishiguro. I managed to find homes for those two articles in midlevel scholarly journals. My plan was to combine my new work on Ishiguro with what I had already done in my dissertation and produce a new book on postwar British fiction.

But that goal, realistically, is a long way off. For this semester all I want is an article out of one chapter of my dissertation.

As I page through that chapter on a Friday morning, sitting on the couch in my basement—a playroom that doubles as my study—I feel a range of emotions upon returning to this document that had occupied so much of my intellectual life and energy for two long years. But my basic reaction, over and over again, is simple disbelief: I wrote *that?*

Sometimes the reaction is a positive one. I am impressed by the range of sources I marshaled to support my argument, and by the thoroughness of my readings of the novels. I am surprised by references to, and long quotations from, articles I have no recollection of reading. But sometimes the reaction is quite negative, as when I came across the portentous and clunky sentence that opens the section I want to extract for an article: "Let me begin my reading of *Black Dogs,* somewhat paradoxically, by trying to situate the novel's critique of purely conventional and rational history within a conventional biographical and socio-cultural historical context."

Oh, Lord. How paradoxical!

The more I read through the chapter with an eye towards cutting it down into a journal article, the more my heart sinks at the realization that this will require much more work than I have the time and energy for. While the chapter's argument is solid and, I think, worth publishing, it relies heavily on the extensive theoretical framework I built up in my introduction. In order to get my reading of this novel down to a length suitable for a journal submission, I would have to condense my thirty-page introduction into a few pages, then cut a good twenty pages from my reading of the novel.

An hour after having sat down with it, I put my dissertation back into its box and set it on a shelf in the basement. That one, I say to myself, will have to wait until break.

3. Ditto my essay on Jeanette Winterson. By the time I get around to teaching her novel, at the end of October, I have completely abandoned any plans to draft an essay during those weeks. The problem, I have discovered, is that embarking upon any sort of scholarly writing—with all the attendant tasks of gathering the background research, reading what I have collected, and planning the essay—requires, at least for me, a series of significant chunks of time. In other words, if I have an hour free, as occasionally happens, I can't just sit down and start writing or outlining. It takes me a few hours to page through my notes and the articles I have

read, reminding myself of the arguments I have to consider, and a few more hours just to think and make new notes. So if I sit down on a Friday with six hours ahead of me, I will just be getting ready to write by the time Katie has to be picked up from kindergarten. If I have two consecutive free days to write, I can shorten the preparation process on the second day to an hour or two, then begin to get some real writing done. But that second day would be Saturday, which I don't have free to write, and then on Sunday I'm back to thinking about my classes again.

It is a hard realization to come to, but one that is crystal clear to me by the end of October: I no longer expect to do any scholarly work during this first semester.

4. What I can sit down and write without much preparatory work are the personal essays that increasingly interest me. Lately, when I have a free hour or two and want to write, this is what emerges on my computer screen. The fit between my schedule and this genre—loosely defined as creative nonfiction—starts me thinking more seriously about this kind of writing.

Many of my academic heroes, literary theorists like Umberto Eco, Edward Said, and Stanley Fish, regularly write nonfiction essays for popular periodicals, and I have always loved reading them. I could do that, I think to myself. Though I can't do scholarly work during the semester, I could write the sort of essays that would define me as a public intellectual.

Over the course of two writing Fridays in late September, I write and revise an essay on the academic job-hunting season, which is in full swing, and describe its Byzantine and protracted stages for a public audience. I read the essay aloud into a tape recorder, send a copy to National Public Radio's *Morning Edition*, and wait for Bob Edwards to call.

What I forget about public intellectuals, especially ones like Umberto Eco, Edward Said, and Stanley Fish, is that they were intellectuals before they were public. They made their academic reputations with works of scholarship that established whole new fields and schools of literary theory, and they each followed those works up with a succession of solid scholarly books—and in Eco's case, bestselling novels.

As the days of October stretch on with no calls from Bob Edwards, I come to realize that the public is not clamoring for the musings of an intellectual whose scholarly work consists of an unpublished dissertation and a couple of articles on postwar British literature published in specialized academic journals.

All of which is to say that, with the sole exception of my *Chronicle* articles, I am either not writing, or not writing anything worth publishing. And maybe this isn't such a big deal. After all, I have five and a half years until my tenure case. Do I really need to be cranking out articles and essays already?

The truth is, I don't know. I will have a first-year review at the end of the year; will they expect to see that I have done at least some publishing by then? I will have a third-year review to start preparing for at the end of my second year; surely I will need to show signs of productivity by then, at the halfway point to tenure? And given the long response times of many academic journals, I feel that I don't have any time to waste.

No one is deliberately hiding this information from me. But the college and the department, like most colleges and departments I know of, take no formal steps to provide junior faculty with this sort of feedback in their first semester. Maybe I could get the information if I pressed someone hard enough, but I don't want to be perceived as needy or lazy. If I ask a senior colleague whether I should be publishing in my first year, will he announce at lunch with his peers the next day that Lang can't seem to handle the workload and is trying to skate by without doing any writing in his first year, and did we perhaps make a mistake with him?

So I keep my head down and my mouth shut and wonder about it.

I wonder about another question as well. If I can't get any writing done during my three-course semester, and I know I won't get any done during my four-course semester, am I going to last in this position?

As I did with my teaching problems, I turn to my colleagues in the department for guidance. I don't really *talk* to anyone about it, again because I don't want my foolish questions to shape their impressions of me. Instead, I try to find out what their publishing track records look like and hope that this will tell me what mine should look like.

As far as I can tell, only one member of the department has published a book. Charles was hired the year before me, from a non-tenure-track position at a large research university in the South. He specializes in contemporary American poetry, and his first book, which will be published in the spring by a midlevel Southern university press, presents the history of a specific poetic form. He has the cover image for the book on his door.

Sometimes I think about going to Charles for advice or to find out how he got his book published, but he is not the most approachable person in the world. He doesn't talk much at meetings, for example, but when he does, it is usually to point out, if diplomatically, the folly of some course of action we are about to agree upon. He intimidates me, to be honest, in the way that a quiet and self-confident person can. He also seems not to have much emotional investment in the college. I rarely see him at extracurricular events. My suspicion (not based on any fact) is that he took the job because he wanted a tenure-track position, but that once his book comes out he will be on the market for better jobs back in the South.

Indeed, this equation seems to explain the publication records of most people in the department. Their publishing output is in inverse proportion to their job satisfaction. Those who seem most happily ensconced at the college, in other words, publish the least; those who seem to want to move on publish considerably more.

Dan, the department poet, works very hard at his poetry. I don't think I have ever met anyone so serious about poetry; he lives and breathes it. One night out at the local bar, where I occasionally went for drinks with Mark, Ed, and Dan, he pulled out a poem called "Cleaning the Well," by Fred Chapell, and read part of it aloud to me before the others arrived: "'Two worlds there are," he intoned in a measured and clearly practiced reading voice, "One you think / You know; the Other is the Well."

I had to resist the urge to sink down into the booth as he declaimed, however much I admired a passion for poetry so strong that its possessor carries it with him to bars. Dan plans to use his sabbatical next year to get his book of poems completed, revised, and submitted to contests and publishers. We live just a few houses down from Dan, and his wife and Anne are friends. She told Anne once that they would definitely consider moving on if Dan's book got published and helped establish his reputation as a poet.

Ed is the one exception to the pattern that those who publish the most seem most likely to test the job market someday. He does very well received, traditional literary scholarship. He is editing the works of an obscure seventeenth-century woman writer and also a collection of essays on one of Shakespeare's plays. He writes book reviews and entries in literary dictionaries as well. Ed, in other words, is a very traditional and productive scholar in a very traditional and productive field. With his popularity as a teacher and his scholarly track record, I imagine that he could easily land a job at a more research-oriented institution.

But Ed's wife, a professor of French literature, has a job at a nearby college, and they are surely aware of their good fortune to be an academic couple with jobs in the same city. If he gets tenure, I don't foresee him ever leaving. Ed, like me, must simply be driven to write, and he has been very successful at it.

Most of the senior faculty are at the other end of the scale. They seem perfectly happy with their jobs and their lives, and write little if at all. They are not intellectual deadwood, by any means; they obviously choose to focus their intellects on the challenges of classrooms and committees. Most of them, though, do have academic or pedagogical projects of one kind or another.

Take the chair of the department, for example. I like her very much. She was especially kind to me during the hiring process and continues to be kind during my first months at the college. Whenever we cross paths, she asks how I am doing and responds promptly and fully to any of my concerns. A devout Catholic herself, she gave me high praise for an essay I had written about being a Catholic academic. She teaches courses in drama, including drama from postwar England, the period in which my own scholarly work has been focused, so she and I have had the occasional conversation about that.

According to her faculty web page, she has not published a scholarly essay since 1981, and that one appeared in a very specialized literary studies journal. But she occasionally mentions research she is conducting on a famous nineteenth-century playwright, and in fact she plans to use her sabbatical next year to travel to visit the archives of this playwright in Norway.

Her good friend in the department, Kim, has a similar track record. I get along equally well with Kim. She was the chair of the search committee that hired me, and her office is next door to mine. Her last publication, an essay in a very reputable journal, was in 1986. But she has clearly not been inactive in the years since then. For one thing, she wrote her dissertation about the literature of Victorian England but now seems to specialize, judging from the classes she teaches, in twentieth-century African-American literature. Obviously she has spent time developing this new expertise. She also makes full use of our generous travel budget—we each get $1,500 per year, a major perk of many small liberal arts colleges—to present papers at conferences across Europe and the United States, work that is certainly legitimate and valuable. Her scholarly travels carry the name of our college around the world and put her in touch with rising scholars and new ideas in her field.

Something I have noticed about both Kim and our chair is that they have full and involved lives off campus. They seem happy and secure in their positions at the college as well as in their private lives. The chair often mentions cultural events she attends in Boston with her husband. Kim actually lives on a farm in a neighboring state. They are also both tenured, of course. So while they both conduct research, they also both seem to have goals and uses for that activity other than publishing in conventional academic modes. Their research gives them opportunities to travel, to explore new fields, and, no doubt, simply to maintain active intellectual lives.

Maybe that's why the necessity to write looms so large in my own mind; I have very little life off campus. I have a wife and children, true, but I seem to be spending less time with them than I used to, and when I am with them, I am usually preoccupied with thoughts of school. Trying to get by on the salaries of a part-time teacher and an assistant professor, Anne and I can't afford to pay a babysitter and go anywhere together except on very rare occasions. Even if we could go out, we haven't been in Worcester long enough to have figured out where to go.

On top of that, I am still battling the symptoms of my Crohn's disease, which has gone into only a very tentative and partial remission. I am still plagued by bouts of diarrhea and fatigue, making the prospect of drives into Boston or the surrounding area for day trips a source of anxiety.

At the start of the semester, in September, it seemed as if people in the department were much more inclined to get together for social occasions both planned and spontaneous. We had a departmental barbecue; we ate dinner one night at Dan's house; a couple of times I went out to a local bar with some of the junior faculty. But now, at midsemester, no one has the time or energy to organize such gatherings. So in addition to feeling worn down by the stresses of our jobs and the adjustments we are still making to a new house in a new city, Anne and I are feeling isolated.

In the past, when I was feeling sick or isolated or anxious about something, I was always able to turn to my writing. Here, at the end of October, that source of solace seems to be slipping away.

In retrospect, what I needed the most at that time was the simple advice that I now would give to anyone about to begin the first year on the tenure track: Do not expect to write anything in your first semester as a full-time faculty member. If you are at a college where teaching matters as much for your tenure as writing does (or more), give yourself the entire year off from writing. If I had heard, and heeded, this advice in my first year, it would have made the single biggest difference—more than any changes I could have made in my teaching or service or home-life commitments—in the quality of my life, in the levels of my stress, and in the management of my time.

If not writing anything at all for long stretches of time makes you unhappy and anxious, as it does me, I would add to my hypothetical advisee, use any writing time you have to plan what you will write during your first break or your first summer. Identify journals to query about writing a book review; look around for annual conferences you might attend in your second year; open a file on your computer called "Writing Goals" and list the projects you would like to complete to help you earn tenure. When you get the itch to write in that first semester, go to that file and write down your ideas. Expect to get back to them over break or, more likely, during the summer.

Even consider writing about the adjustment experience itself. You'll be doing it anyway, believe me, in long and whiny e-mails sent to friends and family about the ways in which you had not bargained for any of this.

At the end of October, frustrated by my inability to write and by the demands that are eating away at my writing time, I fall back upon what I always do when confronted with a problem I can't easily resolve. I write about it.

I title the essay I wrote for the *Chronicle* in October "College Math" and begin it this way:

> When I accepted a tenure-track position as an English professor at a liberal arts college, I didn't realize how much time I would devote to solving complex mathematical problems.
>
> *Question:* If I am teaching three courses this semester, each for a total of two and a half classroom hours a week, and have to spend two to three hours of preparation for each hour in the classroom, in addition to all of the grading; if I have to spend ten hours a week in the office, much of which time I devote to administrative and service responsibilities; if I have one wife plus two children, and spend three half-days a week at home with the children and at least an hour or two in the evening with all four of us together; if I can set aside the 8–11 P.M. block four days a week for working time; and if I want to allow myself at least one hour each day—just one, that's all I need—to relax and watch reruns of *The Simpsons* and *Seinfeld* on late-night television before I collapse in the evening; if all these apply, how many hours does that leave me for my own writing and research?
>
> *Answer:* It depends. How much of my weekend am I willing to sacrifice?
>
> *Extra-Credit Question:* How many hours will I have for my writing next semester, when I am teaching four courses instead of three?

Serving

I hate meetings.

That sentence, actually, doesn't come close to capturing the emotion. To borrow an expression once used by Diane Chambers on the sitcom *Cheers,* I hate meetings with the white-hot intensity of a thousand suns.

During my three years at the Searle Center, meetings were the bane of my existence. My resolution never to return to any sort of administrative role in higher education was forged in the crucible of meetings there. I could have remained happily in that position forever, or at least for a lot longer than I did, if meetings had not formed such a major part of my job.

I had to meet alone with the director, I had to meet with the entire staff of the center, I had to meet with several committees, I had to meet with graduate students. Probably my most important role at the center was planning a workshop—code word for "meeting"—for the new graduate student teachers each year, to introduce them to college-level teaching. The meeting itself, a day-long affair involving several hundred people and dozens of facilitators, required many preliminary planning meetings.

At first I thought it possible that my colleagues felt as I did—that they too, deep down, hated meetings, although they put up a brave front in order to please whatever puppetmasters were creating the issues that required decisions and, hence, meetings. But I learned otherwise one afternoon in my final year at the center when a few of us were sitting in the common room waiting for the director to join us for a meeting.

"I hope this goes quickly," I said, munching on a cookie from the tray just set down by the program director.

"I think the ideal length for a meeting," mused one of my colleagues, a former psychology professor who was now the center's lead researcher, "is about ninety minutes. That's usually enough time to accomplish some real work."

If I hadn't been so stunned, I would have leaped across the table and throttled him.

So while I like to believe that I left the Searle Center for the tenure track because of my love for literature and because I wanted more time to spend with my wife and children, I sometimes suspect that I actually left because I was sick of meetings and wanted never to attend one again.

Naturally, upon arriving at Assumption, I learned that I had three full days of meetings scheduled in the two weeks prior to the start of classes. But I could see that these were one-time meetings that had been called for good reasons: to orient me to my new job and to prepare the department for the accreditation process that the college was about to undergo.

The arrival of this memo in my departmental mailbox was my first indicator that life on the tenure track was not going to be the meeting-free paradise I had imagined:

SCHEDULE OF MEETINGS: FALL SEMESTER 2000
Time: 4:00–5:15

Date	General agenda
8/31 Th.	Tenure and promotion matters (tenured faculty)
9/05 Tues.	Job description for new position
9/13 Wed.	New/old communications program
10/04 Wed.	Spring 2001 course schedule
11/01 Wed.	Search matters
11/28 Tues.	Preparation for accreditation visit

I naively concluded, thanks to some quick math on my part, that the meetings would last an hour and fifteen minutes. By November I begin to suspect that the 4:00–5:15 projected meeting time is someone's idea of a cruel joke. The meetings last anywhere from an hour and a half to over two hours. They never, *ever,* last an hour and fifteen minutes.

I find two things about this particularly irksome. First, we seem to spend the first half-hour chatting, making announcements, and discussing the agenda. This is maddening to me. Surely we could make these announcements more efficiently with an e-mail message or a note dropped into everyone's mailbox?

Second, the meetings take place at a time of day when I am usually looking after the children so that my wife can relax for a bit before preparing dinner. The long meetings continually try Anne's patience. When a meeting progresses beyond 5:15, my mind increasingly drifts to the look of smoldering resentment I will see on her face when I walk through the door.

On the day of my first meeting, it was after six o'clock when I got home and found my family seated at the dinner table. Anne greeted me icily: "Late meeting?"

It was said in a way that communicated something quite different: "So, you had a meeting that lasted until 5:15, and then you decided to hang out in your office chatting with your new colleagues while I had to stay here by myself and make dinner for your children?"

I don't think she believed me about the long meetings until she heard some of my colleagues complaining about them as well.

But the meetings try my patience, too. I like to spend time with my children—playing tag in the front yard with Katie and her friends, or collecting acorns with Madeleine as we saunter up and down our tree-lined street—and these meetings are robbing me of my family time.

Equally annoying, though perhaps more justifiable, is the fact that we all have to participate in *every single decision* the department makes. Our first meeting in September was devoted primarily to writing the job description for an opening we would have in the department next year. Twelve of us spent an hour laboring over what ended up as a fifty-word description. While part of me is glad that we all have an equal voice in such matters, part of me wishes that this were a business and somebody would just make the decisions for us. Twelve of us spent an hour each writing this ad—that's twelve person-hours to come up with fifty words. Couldn't one person have done it, sent it around by e-mail for approval, and made any requested changes?

At 5:45, with no end to the meeting in sight, I sometimes want to shout: Does everything have to be so democratic? Can't someone just take charge and make a decision around here?

But I mustn't overreact. We're talking about just five departmental meetings over the course of the semester, right? I can handle that.

But wait—there's more!

Thanks to the accreditation process the college is undergoing, we are experimenting with a new form of departmentwide assessment in the freshman English courses. In the first week of classes all students in Freshman Composition and Introduction to Literature wrote an in-class essay on a common topic. We used their responses to assess the overall quality of their writing as they entered college. At the end of the semester we will give them another common in-class essay assignment and see how far they have progressed.

In theory, this sounds like a good idea. It seems logical, and such an assessment exercise would probably give us useful information about what we should be doing in our composition classes. But I can already foresee the problem that nobody is addressing: Who the hell is going to have the time to read all those essays at the end of the semester, and what are they going to do with them once they have read them?

Whatever the ultimate fate of the essays, it of course turns out that we must have some meetings to talk about them—three over the course of the semester. Kim has taken charge of this project, and she convenes and leads the meetings. They don't focus entirely on the assessment project. They actually seem more like a chance for us to talk with other composition teachers about ideas for our classes. Someone will describe a problem she is having in class, and the rest of us will listen and commiserate or offer advice. We also talk about techniques that are working well and share those with the group.

I find that sort of idea-exchange interesting, so these meetings leave me feeling a little conflicted. Usually I come away with a useful new idea or two, but in order to get those nuggets I have had to sit through an hour of what, at its worst moments, sounds like a lot of support-group talk.

I am curious about who attends these meetings. At least half of the full-time faculty are teaching composition, but only Charles and I regularly attend the meetings. The other participants are the half-dozen or so adjunct faculty members whom the department has hired to fill out our composition sections. When I get the e-mail announcing the meeting times, it never states or implies that the meeting is optional. So why are all my senior colleagues, and some of my junior ones, skipping these meetings?

Not counting the meetings at the beginning of the semester, we're still talking only eight obligatory meetings over a sixteen-week period. That's only one meeting every other week.

But I'm forgetting about a few others.

On October 17, from 5:30 to 7:30, I have a dinner and informal meeting with the chair of my department, all the other new hires for this year, and the chairs of their departments. At least I get dinner (chicken).

On November 6, the department holds the induction ceremony for Sigma Tau Delta, honoring English majors with GPAs above 3.0. At this event, orchestrated by Ed, we are each asked to say a few kind words about one or two students we know from class. I am to speak about a student from the British fiction class. I enjoy this event. Most of the students have invited their parents, and in some cases siblings and grandparents, and they are wearing dresses or coats and ties. My colleagues perform well for the crowd. They are witty and eloquent, making jokes and showering praise on their favorite students. Pride radiates from the students and their parents, and the evening leaves me with an impression of the department as a genial and tightly knit community of scholars and teachers. Afterwards we stand around and meet the parents, shaking hands and making awkward small talk.

And then there is my meeting with the president of the college to discuss how I am settling in. This is the shortest meeting I will ever attend, a fact that I find both worrisome and a welcome change.

My appointment is scheduled for 1:30 on a Wednesday, meaning that it takes place during my office hours. (Am I supposed to formally cancel and reschedule the missed half-hour?) I show up in the president's office five minutes early and cool my heels in the waiting room, paging through the alumni magazine while his secretary types away. At 1:30 he

calls me in, and we sit across from one another in high-backed, cushy chairs.

The conversation runs as follows:

1:30: Pleasantries

1:31: I tell him that my new sister-in-law's brother-in-law is the brother-in-law of his son—or something like that. I learned this at my brother's recent wedding in October. By the end of my explanation, we're both befuddled.

1:33: He explains to me the purpose of the meeting, to see how I'm adjusting to Assumption and to address any problems or concerns I might have.

1:34: I state that I have no problems or concerns, then babble on for a bit about how I had some difficulty adjusting to the students at first but now I have the hang of it and everything is fine.

1:43: He tells me he is happy to hear it.

1:44: Slightly awkward pause. I wait for the president to move the meeting to its next stage. Then I figure it out: he is waiting for me to leave. I clap my hands together gently, as if finishing something up, and stand. We shake hands, and I leave.

While I am happy to have concluded the meeting so quickly, I wonder if I have committed some kind of presidential-meeting *faux pas*. Was I supposed to talk more? Is there some unwritten code that says faculty members are obliged to carry the conversation in meetings with the president? Did he want me to complain? Did he want me to be more effusive in my praise of all things Assumption?

At the office the next day, on break between classes, I see Mark's door open and go in to tell him about my brief discussion with the president. While Mark is naturally a far more talkative person than I am, I am still going to be a little worried if he tells me that he and the president whiled away an afternoon drinking café lattés and exchanging fraternity stories.

Fortunately, Mark's experience makes me feel considerably better. He completely forgot about his meeting with the president and skipped

it. When he remembered and called the president's secretary, sick with worry, to double-check that he had indeed done what he thought he had done, she replied, "Yes, that's right. You blew off the president."

So things could have been worse—and were worse, of course, for Mark, whose subsequent meeting with the president, when he reschedules it, proceeds just as mine did. But whatever else he may think of me, at least the president knows that I am punctual and can meet my scheduled obligations.

This completes the roster of obligatory meetings during my first semester. It does not, however, complete the overall roster of meetings.

I know vaguely that I am obligated, like all faculty members, to serve on committees, but I don't yet know what these committees are or how one signs up for them. Will someone approach me and ask me to join one? Is it like picking baseball teams when we were kids, with the committee captains picking all the best faculty members first? If I don't get picked, am I the kid nobody wants and who gets stuck out in right field? Or am I supposed to seek out the captains and beg them to let me be on the team?

I don't yet know that committee assignments at my college are made in the spring. The assignments have already been made for the year, but I am under the impression that I must scramble to find some concrete way to demonstrate my commitment to service now, in my first semester.

I figure that the easiest way for me to serve the college would be to help organize meetings at which faculty can exchange ideas about teaching—precisely the sort of meetings I spent three years at the Searle Center organizing. I would feel competent doing this, and since there would be only one or two such meetings to set up during the semester, the work would be far more tolerable than it was at the center, where I worked on dozens a year.

I ask a few people whether other faculty might have an interest in such an activity and discover that one already exists: a faculty teaching colloquium, held two or three times a semester. Three of the organizers of this colloquium are tenured professors in my department.

So I approach one of them—Amy, who teaches Victorian literature. Amy has long gray hair and an air of having been reluctantly pulled from

the sixties. Her door is a collage of postcards, quotations, bumper stickers, and cartoons, all having something to do with peace, social justice, or women's rights and achievements. Even when discussing the most trivial things, she speaks with such sincerity and warmth that I sometimes feel as though we're just one really empathetic remark away from hugging.

Amy welcomes my interest in the colloquium, and when the schedule for the series goes out to the faculty, it has my name at the bottom as one of the committee members.

I even agree to be one of four presenters at the first colloquium, which takes place in October and is entitled "Teaching in the Disciplines." We are each supposed to present an assignment or exercise from our own classes that might be transferable to other disciplines. I decide to talk about my composition course, about case studies, and present the case study I am doing with the students on *Huckleberry Finn.*

When I describe my experiment to the dozen or so faculty members who gather over plates of cheese and fruit that afternoon in October, it once again strikes me—as it did when I was planning it—as an interesting and innovative idea. I don't say much about the fact that the students are not finding it nearly as interesting as I thought they would, or that I am scaling back my original version of the course on the fly. I am supposed to be an expert on teaching, after all, given my experience at the Searle Center, and I don't want everyone to know that my grand experiment is, at best, a noble failure.

Joining the colloquia team gives me opportunities to talk to Amy, and I feel very comfortable with her. Like Kim, she has migrated some from her original field of Victorian literature. She still teaches courses in that area but has a developing interest in postcolonial literature, especially Indian women writers. She has undertaken a long-term collaborative project, with a colleague from another school, editing the letters of a nineteenth-century female British educator for a very reputable scholarly press.

So add two faculty teaching colloquia to the meeting roster. That almost closes it out.

But not quite.

One afternoon in early October, as Mark and I are talking in the hallway, Ed pokes his head out of his office, sees us, and walks over. He

listens to our discussion of the baseball playoffs and contributes a comment or two, but eventually it becomes clear that he has something on his
mind.

"Listen," he finally says. "Please say no if you don't want to do this—
please, really—but I wanted to see if you two would be interested in taking over as advisors for the English Club."

We both shrug and nod.

"What do we have to do?" I ask.

"Hardly anything, if you don't want to. You can be as involved as you
want. The students are supposed to plan all the meetings and events. But
they have to have a faculty advisor, and this will be an easy service commitment for you guys."

This sounds reasonable enough, and we agree to it. Mark and I draft
an e-mail to the current club members, introducing ourselves and sched-
uling an initial meeting for the end of October. We send an e-mail to our
colleagues in English asking them to announce the meeting of the club in
their classes, and I announce it in my classes.

A half-dozen students show up at the meeting, none of whom are in
any of my classes. I recognize one or two from having seen them hanging
around outside Ed's office. Mark has another commitment that prevents
him from being here, so I am the only faculty member present. As they
introduce themselves to me and to each other and talk tentatively about
what the club might do in the upcoming year, I work very hard to repress
the thought that wants to push itself to the forefront of my brain:

These kids are dorks.

Admittedly, "dork" is a relative term. I was no jock or stud in college
myself. Most of my friends were people who liked to spend as much time
as possible at bars and parties but who still had enough interest in literature and ideas to make for interesting conversations and late-night debates. Through my high school and college years I never made it into the
"A" crowd of beautiful people and athletes. I have always been content to
hang with one of the many "B" crowds.

As a student myself, I probably would have looked a little askance at
the sort of students who would join an English Club. But as a faculty
member, I realize that these are the dream students: they probably talk in
class, they care about literature, they want to screen film versions of fa-

mous novels and hold discussions about them—an idea that comes up at the first meeting and that sounds great to me.

The members of the club decide that they need to meet a couple more times during the semester to plan the first event, so they set those times up before we leave.

Ah, well, I sigh to myself as the meeting comes to a close. I'm hanging with the dorks now.

I have one other service obligation that involves working directly with students, one that comes up in November.

At the end of the New Faculty Orientation in August, I had been given five manila folders containing information sheets filled out by five incoming freshmen. I was told that I was the faculty advisor to these students, and that I would need to contact them and set up appointments with them during registration week for the spring semester.

In the first week of November, I follow the lead of my colleagues and send an e-mail message to my five advisees, letting them know that I have taped a piece of paper to my door listing several thirty-minute time slots during the week; they are to come by at their convenience and sign up for an appointment. Two of my advisees are in my composition class, and I remind them about it there. They sign up immediately. Two more names appear on my sheet over the next few days.

One name is missing, and it's the name of the girl I probably most need to speak to. When students are performing at D or F level in a class, we are supposed to send poor-performance notices to their advisors, and to the dean of studies, indicating the precise area in which they are having difficulty. I have received three poor-performance notices for this student, Maggie. "Maggie needs to take the course more seriously," her anthropology professor writes on the notice, "and to put more effort into it, and especially, to come to class. She is clearly capable of much better."

Advising week arrives, with still no word from Maggie. I send her another message but get no response. I should probably pursue the matter more aggressively, get her on the phone, but I always seem to remember her when I don't have time to call, or just don't want to—late at night, early in the morning, five minutes before class.

In the meantime, I meet with my other four advisees for twenty or thirty minutes each. I ask about their experience at Assumption thus far, about their classes, and about their career plans. They seem mostly happy. They speak guardedly about their classes, probably suspecting that I will rush to their professors' offices to report anything critical they say. They have no idea what they want to do with their lives.

I have been very worried about these sessions, because the students are probably as familiar with the course selection process and the requirements for the various majors as I am. If I didn't think it would make me look like a slacker, I would suggest to someone that perhaps I shouldn't be advising anybody just now. But with these kids, advising is relatively simple. They are freshmen, and they have to take four or five general-education core classes each semester. So it's just a matter of finding classes that fit into the most convenient schedule. I feel guilty suggesting that an 8:30 A.M. class will be "most convenient"—I would not have liked to hear that as an undergraduate—but they accept the advice with a resigned shrug, as if they had expected it.

Throughout the four sessions, I become gradually more adept at the advising trick that continues to serve me to this day. If I am not sure about something, I run from the office, advising sheet in hand, and find a senior colleague who can tell me what I need to know. He or she is always happy to help, and every time I ask a question about a student's schedule or courses, I learn something new myself. By the end of the four sessions I feel almost competent to advise.

On the final day of advising week, the Friday before course selection begins, I am sitting in my office grading papers. I have a stack of forty to return by Tuesday, and my Friday writing day has fallen victim to the paperload. I hear a tentative knock on my door and call, "Come in."

The door opens to reveal an unkempt girl with straggly blond hair and a nose ring. She is holding a course catalog and an advising form.

"Um," she says, smiling sheepishly, "I think you're my advisor? I'm Maggie?"

She intones her own name as a question, as if she either needs me to affirm her identity or expects me to break into song at her much-anticipated arrival.

"Yes, yes, come in," I say and motion her to sit down. "I sent you a message last week to sign up for a time. Didn't you get it?"

"Um, no," she says. "I don't check my Assumption e-mail."

"You probably should," I say, more sententiously than I would like. "They send out official announcements and stuff to that account."

"Yeah . . . ," she says, trailing off.

"Well, let's talk about your schedule. First of all, how are things going for you so far?"

She shrugs. "OK."

"Do you like your classes? I saw you were having trouble in a couple of them."

"They're OK."

We go back and forth like this for a minute or two, and then I start to get annoyed. I'm trying to help this girl, but she obviously has no interest in the process. It's like trying to make a permanent impression on a beanbag chair.

I give it one last shot.

"So what do you want to do with your life, Maggie?" I ask.

"I don't know. Maybe write children's books."

"Well, we don't exactly have a major for that here." I pause, not wanting to sound unhelpful. "But maybe you could take studio art or a writing class."

"OK."

At that point, my aggravation level at its peak, I give up. We quickly fill out her schedule—I take the form from her and fill it out myself—and I send her on her way. I don't realize it at the time, but Maggie is a specific student type, one that I will run across at least once or twice a year. She has been sent here by her parents and enjoys the college lifestyle—late hours, late mornings, drinking, hanging out in the dorms—but doesn't want to be in the college classroom, perhaps because she senses she doesn't belong there. She will be gone by the end of the year.

That evening, thinking back on my meeting with her, I feel guilty and vow to help her more effectively next semester.

One final service obligation that I agreed to in August comes due at the end of November. At the departmental retreat an announcement had been made asking for volunteers to serve on the search committee. This committee appealed to me for two reasons: I wanted to help hire an outstanding colleague, and I thought it would provide useful fodder for my *Chronicle* columns. The opportunity to sit behind the interview table for the first time after my recent experiences in front of it should enable me, I think, to give concrete advice to job seekers on how to improve their chances.

So I volunteered. Kim, the chair of the search committee, announces at a later meeting that I am on the committee. I have no idea how or why I was chosen. I don't puzzle about it much until Mark tells me later that he volunteered for the committee before I did and was silently passed over. Who favored me over him, and why?

At the end of November the search committee sets up two meeting times for early December, to winnow through the many dozens of applications that have come in by the November 15 deadline, and to identify a dozen candidates for telephone interviews to be conducted in early January. We are each assigned two ranges of the alphabet and are to look over the folders of candidates whose last names begin with letters in that range. Each range is to be looked at by two of the five members of the committee. We are to pick out the best candidates from our ranges, and at our meetings in December we will compare notes and work to identify the lucky dozen.

I end up enjoying this committee's work almost as much as the best moments of my teaching and writing. The work feels important to me, consequential. We are hiring someone who might, over the course of a long career, change the future of this institution. I also enjoy the pleasant thought of making some job candidate as happy as I was to receive my first tenure-track offer. And since all search committees include one or two faculty members from outside the hiring department, this committee gives me the opportunity to interact with two faculty members from other departments (in this case, biology and education). I've noticed that junior faculty in particular tend to hang out with people from their own department, so I welcome the chance to meet some new faces from across the college.

So here is the final schedule of meetings, in the fall semester of 2000, for the job I had taken in the hope of avoiding meetings:

Thursday, August 17, 9 A.M.: New Faculty Orientation

Tuesday, August 22, 9 A.M.: Departmental retreat

Wednesday, August 23, 9 A.M.: Departmental retreat

Tuesday, September 5, 4 P.M.: Departmental meeting

Friday, September 8, 4 P.M.: Departmental party at a senior faculty
member's house

Wednesday, September 13, 4 P.M.: Departmental meeting

Wednesday, October 4, 4 P.M.: Departmental meeting

Wednesday, October 11, 4 P.M.: Meeting of composition faculty

Thursday, October 12, 4 P.M.: Faculty teaching colloquium

Tuesday, October 17, 5:30 P.M.: Dinner with department chairs and
new faculty

Thursday, October 19, 6 P.M.: English Club

Thursday, October 26, 6 P.M.: English Club

Monday, October 30–Friday, November 3: Meetings with advisees

Wednesday, November 1, 1:30 P.M.: Meeting with the president of
the college

Monday, November 6, 7 P.M.: Sigma Tau Delta induction ceremony

Tuesday, November 7, 4 P.M.: Meeting of composition faculty

Tuesday, November 14, 4 P.M.: Faculty teaching colloquium

Wednesday, November 15, 4 P.M.: Departmental meeting

Thursday, November 16, 7 P.M.: D'Alzon lecture: "Lost in the Cosmos"

Tuesday, November 28, 4 P.M.: Departmental meeting

Thursday, November 30, 6 P.M.: English Club

Wednesday, December 6, 1 P.M.: Search committee meeting

Friday, December 8, 4:30 P.M.: Holiday reception at president's house

Tuesday, December 12, 10:30 A.M.: Composition faculty meeting

Wednesday, December 13, 1 P.M.: Search committee meeting

I knew coming in that I would not be exempt from committee work
and meetings, but I had imagined I would have more control over the
number and nature of the service obligations I undertook. Mindful of
my experience at the Searle Center, I had decided in advance that I would
agree only to those service obligations that I was actually interested in.
And I adhered to that principle: I certainly was interested in the teaching colloquia, the search committee, and the English Club.

But it didn't occur to me that those obligations would come on top of departmental meetings, curricular meetings like those held for composition instructors, meetings with advisees, and—an obligation that will grow more burdensome with each passing year, as students become more comfortable and familiar with you—writing letters of recommendation.

Nobody tells you how much service you are supposed to do, and in a way it's in everyone's best interest not to tell you. If you don't know whether you need to devote more time and energy to service, you are more likely to agree to new assignments than if you are confident about your track record. But if I had to do it again, I wouldn't take on more than one service obligation or committee assignment during my first semester, and I wouldn't accept more than two during my entire first year.

Of course, even if you stick to this reasonable plan, there is a wild card that comes in the form of lectures, panel discussions, performances, and other events you really have no obligation to attend but are likely a part of what pulled you into this profession in the first place. At Northwestern I received advertisements for events like these every day, and I tried to attend several per quarter. It made me feel like part of an intellectual and artistic community.

I had assumed that such events would not be so prevalent on Assumption's smaller campus, but I turned out to be wrong.

Throughout the semester I have seen many advertisements for performances, lectures, debates, and discussions—evidence of a vibrant intellectual life on campus for those who wish to take advantage of it. In this first semester I have taken advantage of it only one time—but it proved to be well worth it.

The college sponsors four lectures per year on philosophical or religious topics, given by the endowed chair at the college—a senior scholar in any field, usually philosophy or theology, who teaches one course per semester for a two-year term—or by a distinguished visiting scholar. On November 16 I attend a lecture entitled "Lost in the Cosmos" by the school's endowed chair. The lecture, clearly aimed at undergraduates—many of whom are in attendance, some perhaps nudged there by the promise of extra credit from their theology or philosophy professors—offers a broad philosophical picture of the modern world and advice on how to find our place in it. Because it is aimed at undergraduates, I am able to follow it easily, and while I don't agree with the speaker's conclusions, I find them well articulated and clearly established.

Afterwards I see some colleagues from my department, and some others from philosophy and theology whom I would like to know better. We stand around and talk about the lecture for a bit, and I feel as if I have managed to get my head above water for an instant, long enough to catch a glimpse of the bigger picture and take a gulp of air before slipping under again. A good clear argument, one that I can puzzle over and debate in my mind or with others, followed by discussion afterwards—these are the life-giving elements of the profession I have chosen. I won't get many more gulps of air this year, I know; I just don't have time. But I am hopeful that this will change.

So in that first year, while you are doing your best to keep at bay new commitments to service and committee work, take time out for at least one lecture, one debate, one performance—something outside your field or discipline, something that offers you a momentary taste of that clear, clean air above.

And a final piece of advice, from my fourth-year perspective. If you find yourself stuck in meetings for half of your week because you have been bullied into accepting more service assignments than you can handle, or because you are hoping that an exemplary service record will make up for your failings as a teacher and writer, I would encourage you to do as I have learned to do in meetings.

I bring a notepad and a pencil and all the paperwork that attends the matter we are discussing. I take only bottled water; I am far too serious about the meeting for cookies and fruit. I always—and this is absolutely key—find a seat at the corner of the table. I write the date and the title of the committee, large and legibly, at the top of my notepad, for all to see.

Then, as the meeting begins, I lean back in my seat, legs crossed, notepad resting on my thigh, and quietly work on my lesson plans.

Grading

The first essay assignment for my composition students, back in September, asked them to describe, in the form of a personal narrative, a work of art that had influenced their lives in some way. "Your narrative essay," the assignment sheet explained, "should describe the experience you had *(what happened?)*, offer some explanation as to why that piece of art had such an impact upon you *(why did it happen?)*, and explain what you learned from that personal experience *(what did it mean?)*."

I must confess that my initial reaction, upon receiving the completed papers, was one of relief: the essays weren't nearly as bad as I had expected them to be.

For the past seven years I had been studying or teaching at an institution that regularly ranked in the top twenty colleges or universities in the nation, as the university's promotional magazine never shied from reminding us. I suppose I had bought into the hype by the time I left and imagined that the students I would find at Assumption would be vastly inferior. It will take me most of my first year to understand that many of these students are as intellectually capable as the best students at Northwestern, and that many of them chose a school like Assumption for reasons other than its academic ranking: because of its Catholic character, or because of its proximity to their home, or because they wanted the personalized attention they would receive at a small college. So many of my students, I will realize, could have made the grade at a school like Northwestern; for their own reasons, often personal or familial or financial ones, they simply elected not to.

I didn't yet know this when I received that first batch of papers, so I was pleased to see that most of the students were competent writers. They could put together a sentence, they could form coherent paragraphs, they could even occasionally turn an interesting phrase. From the silences I had been encountering in the classroom, I had expected much worse.

Not to say, of course, that the pile didn't contain some clunkers. One of those came from Mary, a tall and especially quiet student. The few times during the semester I have called on Mary, she has literally frozen with fear. She tries to make herself as invisible as possible to me—which is difficult, given her height. Mary's essay began like this:

> The personal experience I had was based on two events. These events a *[sic]* different yet they have a lot in common. One of these events hit me harder because I knew the kid who did this bad thing it happened in my hometown.

Never mind the typographical and grammatical errors, the bland word choices, and the meaningless sentences; Mary had chosen to write about watching a special edition of NBC's *Dateline*. And while I enjoy Stone Phillips as much as the next guy, that stretched the boundaries of even my very loose definition of a work of art.

One or two essays stood out on the other end of the spectrum as well, like one student's description of how her reading of *Angela's Ashes* inspired her to undertake volunteer work. The memoir, she wrote, made her feel as if she "were right there with him picking pieces of coal up off the street to warm his house." She grasped the assignment clearly, fulfilled it effectively, and wrote a very readable paper. It earned her a B-plus, which is the highest grade anyone earns on this assignment; I don't give out a single A.

I don't give out any D's or F's either, though.

Ben, with the Red Sox cap, received the lowest grade in the class, a C-minus. For an assignment that asked for a three- to four-page paper on the influence a work of art had had on him, Ben wrote a one-and-a-half-page paper about watching the Boston Bruins play hockey. And while I have seen sophisticated theoretical arguments claiming that a sporting event constitutes a kind of drama, Ben wasn't making that argument. He just wanted to write about hockey. His paper included gems like this one: "Growing up watching sports always makes you want to be like somebody." Like the plumber? Like the president? Like Steve Martin in *The Jerk*, inspired by a magazine advertisement to "Be Somebody"?

In truth, Ben's paper deserved a D or even an F. But here at the close of my first semester, I have yet to give out a single D or F. I have handed out plenty of C's, especially in the two composition classes. Nineteen of thirty-three students, in fact, received some form of a C on that first narrative essay. But I haven't yet been able to bring myself to put that D or F on a paper.

There are several reasons for this.

In my first couple of years as a graduate student, I taught composition classes and served as a teaching assistant in large lecture courses. For the past three years, though, while I was working at the Searle Center and teaching just one course per year, the department allowed me to propose and teach only upper-level courses for majors. In the three years I taught those classes, I may have given out one C as a student's final grade for the course (maybe; I'm not even certain about that). I probably gave out less than a handful of C's on *all* the papers I graded in those three years.

Of course, those students were highly competitive. Their grades would earn them positions at prestigious companies or admission to law school or medical school. If I had put a C on an English major's paper at Northwestern, it would probably have sent the student into a seizure; a D or an F would probably have earned me a lawsuit. But I don't think I was an easy grader, by any means. Those students were majors, they were mostly juniors and seniors, and they were smart and independent. Many of them were very talented writers, and some wrote papers that were as sophisticated and intelligent as work that an advanced graduate student might have produced.

That first batch of papers in composition at Assumption were certainly not of the quality I had been accustomed to receiving, but then again, this was a required general-education course for freshmen, as opposed to an upper-level course for majors. I had been told by a colleague to grade harshly, in order to let these freshmen know that they were now writing to different standards than in high school, but I hesitated to judge these students by the standards I had used at Northwestern in those upper-level classes. That hesitation kept me from grading anyone too harshly, and from handing out the few D's or F's that first batch deserved.

A second, less noble reason, though, is also preventing me from giving out D's and F's: I want my students to *like* me, and I'm afraid that if I give out D's and F's, they will think I am a jerk.

Why do I want them to like me so much? I don't know. I don't want to hang around with them at the bars, and I don't especially enjoy talking to them in my office (as I've noticed Ed and Mark, for example, seem to do). I am not this needy for approval in other areas of my life. I don't walk around the neighborhood looking forlornly into people's windows, hoping they will come out and chat with me, and I have never been the sort to disparage myself in the hopes that others will respond with effusive praise and compliments.

But I *really* want my students to like me.

I can think of only one explanation for this strange feeling. I have been doing this job for just about an entire semester now, and nobody in a supervisory role has given me any sort of feedback on my teaching. This makes perfect sense, since nobody has observed me teaching. But since nobody has told me how well I am teaching, and since I have no way to measure myself against my colleagues, the students are my only indicators. In a sense, then, I only have one group of people who, in December, are capable of telling me whether I am a good professor.

And I really, *really* want them to like me.

So I seem to have offered them an unwritten contract: everybody like me, and I won't give out any D's or F's.

This sentiment is probably coloring the grades in British fiction even more than in composition. These are the majors, after all, the people I might see again in future classes. Only a handful of the students in my composition class will become majors, so most of them I will never see in class again. I've heard from colleagues that at a small school like ours, especially when some of us regularly teach the required major courses, students in the major may show up in our classes two, three, even four times over the course of their four years. So how these kids feel about me won't just affect my evaluations; it will also determine the faces I'll be seeing in my classrooms over the next couple of years.

The grades have been deservedly higher in this course than in com-

position, because most of these students are majors, and they are definitely more competent writers than the freshmen. I've given out only
one or two C's on the papers. As the semester goes on and I continue to
hand out B's and A's, I begin to see that I am grading too leniently. But
even though I know this, it seems unfair to change the standards in the
middle of the semester.

I know what these students are capable of, and that I should hold them
to the highest standard, because of Margaret. Margaret has continued to
hand in absolute works of art—beautifully written papers with insightful
analysis of the works we are reading. I had a brief suspicion, after her first
paper, that a paper this good might be plagiarized, but no. Her subsequent
work and classroom contributions have disabused me of that notion.
After having seen the first of her papers, I began calling on her more
frequently, and now she occasionally participates in the discussions of her
own accord. I appreciate Margaret too because no matter how badly I
think I am failing in the class, and no matter how long she goes without
speaking, she always seems attentive and interested. Margaret is the easiest student I have to grade in the class. She has straight A's.

The most difficult student I have to grade is Joanne. Joanne is wonderful to have in class. She clearly does the reading, and she will always
add her voice to the discussion. But she is still, at this stage of her academic career (she is a junior), struggling with her writing. And what she
lacks in skill, to my sorrow, she more than compensates for in determi-
nation.

Having earned a B on her first two short papers—they are writing six
short papers in all, as well as longer midterm and final papers—Joanne
came to see me in my office a few days before the third paper was due.

"Would you mind looking at this for me," she asked, "and telling me
what I can do to make it better?"

"Sure," I told her. "Have a seat."

As she sat watching me read her paper, I became increasingly uncomfortable and increasingly uncertain of how to handle the situation.
While I could certainly help her correct the grammatical errors and could
probably improve some of her more awkward phrasing, I didn't know
how to explain to her that she was making a very obvious point about the

novel, one that would never make for an A paper however much she fancied it up.

But we spent fifteen minutes talking about the paper anyway, me doing my best to push her towards some new idea or insight, she focused as much as possible on finding out how to improve and correct the paper she had already written. When she handed the paper in a couple days later, I saw all of the specific changes we had discussed in terms of the writing, along with the same old obvious idea.

But how do I explain to this girl that, despite her initiative in coming to see me, and despite the work we did together on the paper, it still is B work at best? I think about it for a while and decide that I can't. Feeling like a coward and a fraud, I put an A on it and do my best to forget about it.

Unfortunately, this scenario occurs again and again throughout the semester with Joanne. She now brings me every one of her papers in advance, and we go over them together, with about the same results. I keep giving her A's and keep feeling guilty about it. The truth is, even by my lax standards, Joanne just does not have the writing talent—at least at this stage of her education—to do A work in my class. I know I am doing something wrong in giving her those A's but I also know that I just don't have the energy to fight with her about the grades if I give her what she deserves.

And besides, I want her to *like* me.

Grading is a much simpler proposition with another talkative student, Teri, who volunteered first on that first day of class. I like Teri a lot. She is funny, she never hesitates to volunteer in class, but she also knows when to keep her mouth shut and let other people talk. Sometimes, before class starts, she will ask me questions not related to the class, and sometimes she will chat with other students about her weekend or her personal life in a way that seems to invite me into the conversation. I can tell she is trying to distract me and postpone the beginning of class, but I don't particularly mind.

Teri writes B papers and seems perfectly content with that. She came to see me in my office one time—not with a finished product like Joanne, but with a notebook page that had a few ideas sketched on it. She had obviously just finished a cigarette; the smell of smoke filled my office. We talked about her idea for a bit, and then she stood to leave, smiled, and said something like, "I'll write it up, get my B from you, and be happy."

Teri, I will come to recognize, is another well-defined type. She enjoys the college lifestyle very much—the socializing, the parties, the hours, and even some of the classes—but unlike Maggie, she is savvy enough to know that she has to maintain her grades in order to preserve that lifestyle. She doesn't strive for A's. She has no interest in competing with those around her for grades. She just wants to enjoy college.

Her attitude at first strikes me as bizarre, no doubt because it is so foreign to me, so unlike my own ambition. While I too enjoyed the college lifestyle, I also wanted A's—on everything, all the time. At Notre Dame, where I did my undergraduate work, and at St. Louis University and Northwestern, where I earned my two graduate degrees, almost everyone else was just like me. I'm not sure I encountered any Teris.

This is probably the final reason I have been so reluctant to give out low grades. I assume that the students will respond to a low grade the way I would have responded: with shock, anger, and depression. I would also have been arrogant enough to think that any professor who gave me a low grade was obviously an idiot.

I don't want to inspire those emotions in people, and I certainly don't want them thinking I am an idiot. But as the semester progresses and I encounter several students like Teri, and as I hand back all those C papers in composition and the students still come and contribute to class just as they had before they got the papers back, I start to realize that not all the students here—at least in terms of their competitive focus on grades— are like me.

It is early December, the end of the semester, and I have fifty final papers to grade—all of them research papers eight to ten pages long. The composition students had to research and write about a topic of their choosing; the British fiction students had to write a comparative analysis of two or three novels, supported by research in the appropriate literary criticism.

Despite the length of the papers, I imagine that the grading will go quickly because I won't have to write the long responses I devote to each paper during the semester. When I was in graduate school, one of my professors would give full-page typed responses to the papers we turned in. I was impressed and flattered by this; in order to write such a response, he must have taken me seriously as a thinker and a writer. So I vowed to do the same for my students. All semester I have been typing up half-page single-spaced responses to their papers, in addition to the comments I write in the margins.

Half-page, at least, was the goal. But I type very quickly and sometimes find that I have written a full page of comments without even realizing it. I set myself the goal of turning around each paper in ten to twelve minutes, but that goal has eluded me all semester, and I have found myself spending as long as twenty or twenty-five minutes responding to a single paper.

But now, at the end of the semester, I don't have to do that. Someone told me that students almost never come back the next semester to pick up their final papers or exams. If someone does, you just tell her you left it at home, then write up the comments and send it to her a few days later.

Grading these final papers, though, still progresses slowly. I sit up late at a small writing desk in the guest bedroom, papers stacked on the floor to either side of me. I take a paper from one pile, grade it, then throw it into the other pile. I set little goals for myself: grade five papers, then take a break and have a snack. As the grading progresses, I set more limited goals, and continue not to meet them: instead of grading four papers for a ten-minute break, grade three for a thirty-minute break with a snack and a catnap.

I had set the due date for both sets of papers as December 12, the Tuesday of final-exam week. My intention was to do all of the grading and turn in my final grades by that Friday so that I could begin working on the research and writing projects I had neglected for most of the semester. Friday comes and goes with fewer than half of my papers graded, and it is nearly noon the next Tuesday—half an hour before the absolute final deadline—when I finally walk my grades over to the registrar's office and hand them in.

I have another two hours before Anne and Katie will be finished with school, and I should probably stay and start cleaning up my office. It looks as if someone has taken a huge bin of recycled paper and dumped it here. Spread across every flat surface—desk, bookshelves, table, file cabinets, even the floor—is the accumulated paperwork of a semester.

But I am too tired. I go home and take a nap.

As I tend to do with everything, I made ambitious plans for my first real break on the tenure track. After allowing myself a few days to rest, I intended to write the academic conference paper for the abstract I had finally sent to my friend in October; I intended to write a proposal for a new course in creative nonfiction, to meet the deadline for new course proposals in early February; I intended to work on the Ian McEwan and Jeanette Winterson essays and to start putting together the prospectus for my book.

I also intended to start keeping a sort of teaching journal, in which I would write down the techniques that worked and those that failed, the books that worked well and those that didn't, and anything else that might help me when I taught these courses the next time around—as I fully expected I would do within the next year or two. I intended, in other words, to grade my own teaching performance during my first semester and use my comments to help me improve future courses.

With one exception—the new course proposal—I do not accomplish any of the objectives I have set myself for the break. And the reason for this is simple: in both body and brain, I am just too damned tired.

The last thing in the world I want to do, after I hand in those grades, is think about my teaching. I want to put the semester far behind me, forget about it, and move on. And I just cannot bring myself to pull out that dissertation, or the Jeanette Winterson novel I just finished teaching a month or two ago.

My physical tiredness stems in part from the rigors of the semester, but it stems too from the chronic illness that I have been battling all semester, and that takes a sudden turn for the worse at the end of the semester. Crohn's disease, with which I was diagnosed four years ago, is an autoimmune disorder that causes periodic eruptions of inflammation and hemorrhaging in the intestinal tract. Those eruptions happen seemingly at random, or at least for reasons that doctors don't understand. They can last for weeks or months or years at a time. When the disease is inactive, though, I have no symptoms at all.

For most of the semester I have been dealing with low-grade disease activity. I am in the bathroom four or five times per day, I occasionally see blood in the toilet, and I am anemic and almost always tired. In December I begin to see blood more frequently, to make eight or ten trips to the bathroom per day—sometimes I have to scurry out of class and to the nearest restroom while the students are doing a writing exercise or group work—and to suffer a constant case of dehydration. I can still function normally, and I don't look or act sick, but I prefer not to leave the house, because I never know when I am going to need to find a bathroom on short notice. I see my doctor, and we try a new combination of medicines to help get the disease under control. But the remedies always take time, and the best I can hope for is to be healthy again by the start of spring semester.

So instead of launching new scholarly writing projects and grading my performance in my first semester, I end up doing some of the following:

I read the first Harry Potter novel. I like it. I read Jane Austen's *Northanger Abbey*. Like that, too.

I watch a sporting event from start to finish—the first time I have done that since August. The fact that this particular event was a college football bowl game in which my undergraduate alma mater, Notre Dame, is cruelly humiliated by a clearly superior team detracts only slightly from my enjoyment of the event. Not once during the game do I feel guilty about a stack of papers waiting for me in the basement—a blessed relief from the past three months.

I do every load of laundry in the house for four weeks.

I play with my kids every afternoon. I buy them each a set of Tinker Toys for Christmas and teach them how to make dogs, cats, and skyscrapers with pulleys.

I take naps.

I answer the e-mail correspondence I have been neglecting over the semester, then send e-mails to the friends and colleagues with whom I have lost touch since the semester started. I let most of them know that I will probably not correspond again until the summer.

I balance the checkbook.

I pick up Katie from kindergarten every day for three weeks, watching her come skipping down the stairs and out into the snowy playground, talking and laughing with her friends, scanning the crowd for me and then smilingly pretending not to see me. I make her lunch every day and write little notes to her on the napkins I put in her lunchbox.

My thoughts during the break are never far from my physical condition, and eventually, one evening, I sit down and begin writing the story of how the disease has been affecting me over the past several months. I find great satisfaction in telling the story of my disease, and I start thinking about a work of creative nonfiction about the lessons my malfunctioning body has forced me to learn. I draft a proposal and the first two chapters. Since I am just telling my own story, the writing comes easily and quickly.

When the student evaluation forms for my three classes come to me in early January, they jolt me into the realization that I haven't thought about teaching at all for the past three weeks. When I handed out the evaluation forms in late November, I was very curious, and a little apprehensive, about what the students would have to say. I planned to take their comments and summarize them in my teaching journal, making them part of my ongoing effort to improve my teaching. A month after the semester is over, though, these evaluations feel far more like a summative judgment—the final word on a closed and finished product—than part of an ongoing process.

I find the evaluations in a campus envelope in my mailbox on the day Anne and Katie have returned to school, and I take them back to my office to read. I rip the envelope open to find each class's reactions divided into two parts: first, a series of questions that they responded to on a scale of 1 to 5, beneath which are printed the percentages of students who responded with each number; and then typed versions of the students' handwritten responses to some very general questions about my teaching.

I am immediately relieved by the numbers, which are mostly all good—even in the 8:30 class. The questions are designed so that positive answers fall into the "Strongly Agree" and "Agree" categories, and 90–95 percent of the answers, in all three classes, fall into those categories. The only question that earns more than one or two responses outside those categories is the one about my grading. Good God, I wonder, how lenient do you have to be on the grading not to lose points in that category?

But the written responses are what interest me the most. Some of the students clearly take the forms seriously and provide feedback on how I could improve the course.

For example, I had added two additional in-class essay assignments to the two that were required by our departmental efforts at assessment. I did this because I thought it would help the students become more comfortable writing in class, and the final essay would therefore more accurately reflect any improvements in their writing over the course of the semester. But I receive many comments that confirm what I had already begun to suspect: that the in-class essay assignments felt forced and artificial, and that the students learned very little from them. Well, that seems like an easy fix: no more in-class essay assignments in composition.

Equally useful are the comments that point to specific activities that were helpful to students. In response to the question about the most positive aspects of the class, the students point most consistently, I am happy to see, to my extensive comments on their papers. I feel validated and vow to continue that practice—while still doing my best to streamline it.

The forms contain plenty of unhelpful comments, of course. For example, at least half of the students in the 8:30 class complain about the fact that it was an 8:30 class, in comments like this: "I don't think I would make any changes except for the time. It is too early in the morning to think about English." I agree with that sentiment. It *was* too damned early in the morning to think about English.

Other comments, frankly, just don't make sense: "If writing isn't your strong point you suffer from the grade." Well, it *was* a writing class.

Equally worrisome, and a little embarrassing, are the comments stating how much the student has learned, expressed in sentences containing spelling and grammar errors: "I have definately [sic] become a better writer," one student says.

In the end, the comments are mostly positive, and a handful are very flattering. At least a half-dozen students in the British novel class name that course as the best one they have taken at Assumption, and one student actually makes a plea in my behalf to the administration: "Professor Lang is a great addition to the English Dept. He brings a fresh, new perspective, which I think is needed. Great job—keep him at Assumption!" But comments like this next one mean the most to me, because I'd had serious doubts throughout the semester as to whether I was actually making any kind of impression on them: "In high school I learned nothing in my English class. I can say I actually learned something, and I feel it showed through my work. Thank you."

As with the midterm surveys I collected in October, I find the mostly positive nature of the reviews both exhilarating and baffling. While all three classes did improve over the course of the semester, I still felt that I had spent the entire time reaching down their throats to drag out their one-sentence responses to my questions. I saw the discussions as going from awful to mediocre, at best. But the students, again as at midsemester, saw something quite different. "Prof. Lang presented an atmosphere which promoted discussion," one student writes on the end-of-the-semester form. "We had great talks," says another.

I make a few mental notes about changes I can make to specific activities, like the in-class essays and the group work. I am still too tired to write them down, though. I'll start that teaching journal in May, when I have the entire first year under my belt.

In early January, as I begin to make my preparations for the spring semester and banter about New Year's resolutions is in the air, one resolution about teaching and three resolutions about grading in the next semester form themselves in my mind.

First, stick to my strengths. Even when I think I am failing, most students still appreciate the fact that I am talking *to* them, not at them, and that I want to hear what they have to say. Falling into lecture mode would have made my semester much easier, but it wouldn't have been me. I will keep trying to promote discussion and vary activities as much as possible.

Second, do my best not to worry about whether students like me. I don't want them to like me because I'm an easy grader; I want them to like me because I'm a good teacher, whatever grades I give them. Remember that not all the students at this college are as obsessed with grades as I was. Remember too that honest assessments of their work, and the grades that go with those assessments, are ultimately more likely to inspire hard work and learning. So give at least one D or F. If I can just bring myself to do it one time, I am sure it will get easier. Someone, out of the almost eighty students I have on my class lists for next semester, is going to write a D or F paper, and that person is going to get what he deserves.

Finally, don't worry about how other people grade. I have several times tentatively pressed my colleagues into talking about grades, trying to determine whether I should be giving out a certain number of C's or B's or achieving a certain grade-point average. No one has ever been willing to be specific, and I got plenty of mixed messages: grading philosophies appear to be all over the map in the department, and to vary from department to department.

This seems to be true in the profession as a whole, according to the literature on grading I had read at the Searle Center. I have some pretty set ideas about teaching, usually ideas based on research and tested out in my classroom, but I have seen so many conflicting arguments about grading, none ultimately convincing, that I have never settled on a philosophy. I mentioned this one afternoon in the hallway to Laura, one of my senior colleagues.

Laura had been one of the two faculty members who conducted my telephone interview back in January, and during that interview she and I had discovered a significant coincidence: she had attended St. Mary's College (like my wife), and her husband had attended Notre Dame (like me). That personal connection has paved the way for a good working relationship. Laura likes to talk, and whenever I am puzzled about something, I know I can count on her to give it her fullest attention—sometimes so full that I have to break away to get to class or another obligation. She has been extraordinarily kind to me, and I have also discovered that she runs a totally interactive and experimental classroom, one fueled by her interest in interactive classroom technologies. So I respect her opinion very much.

When I broached the subject of my puzzlement at the grading situation with her, she responded with a comment that made sense to me: "Grades are like teaching styles. We are never going to be all the same, and that's just fine. Students will benefit from exposure to different styles and different philosophies. It forces them to think about their education a little bit."

Struck by the wisdom of this, I decided that I needed to figure out my grading philosophy, stick with it, and not worry about how it stacked up against the rest of the department. As long as I make my policy clear to the students, and as long as it is reasonable and fair, I must give them the grades I think they deserve and stand by them.

I feel strengthened in this conviction by a final realization: the responses I received from the students—their grading of me—have helped me understand the importance of providing honest feedback, negative as well as positive. I am happy to receive their praise and heartened by it to continue working on my teaching. But if I had received nothing but praise, I would have been disappointed. I know the semester was not perfect, and I need their help figuring out how to make my courses more effective learning experiences. So I appreciate the constructive criticism as much as the plaudits.

If I am to take my students seriously as learners, as I hope they are taking me seriously as a teacher, I owe them the same honest assessment of their work.

Hiring

In January and early February 2001, the English faculty engages in a battle for the soul of the department.

My understanding of the nature of this battle comes about slowly and doesn't fully emerge until the meeting we hold in early February to vote on the candidates we have interviewed for a new tenure-track position. At that time, and for the first time, I see clearly the fault lines that define two very different camps in the department, each of which sees their candidate as the one who will help build the kind of department, and college, in which they want to spend their careers.

Kim is serving as the search committee chair. She also chaired the search committee that hired me, so I am happy to be serving with her.

I am happy as well to be serving with Maurice, the department's elder statesman and the one faculty member everyone likes and trusts. White-haired, white-bearded, tall, and bespectacled, Maurice looks the part of the elder statesman. He wears jackets and ties in the classroom, and flannel shirts and oxfords on office-hour days. He has joined us for a beer a time or two, hosted a departmental barbecue at his home in the fall, and knows absolutely everything about the college and its history.

He should. Maurice has been at the college in one capacity or another for forty years, from his own days here as an undergraduate through his entire career as a faculty member, including a stint as chair of the department. He cares deeply about the students, perhaps because he once sat where they sit. In the fall, when the college was presenting the budget at an annual meeting for faculty and staff, Maurice stood and questioned a proposed tuition increase, reminding everyone that it would be borne on the backs of our students' families. I felt guilty when I heard this. The potentially devastating effect of tuition increases on our students' families hadn't occurred to me; I was selfishly focused on the size of the raise it would translate into for me. (The fact that one-third of our students are first-generation college students, and that many come from working-class families, hadn't sunk in yet. This was decidedly not the demographic of the average Northwestern student.) Maurice strikes me as he certainly strikes everyone, as a good-hearted person, and he has always been warm and open with me.

In addition to the representatives from our own department, our search committee is required to have at least one member from outside the department. So Maurice, Kim, and I are working with Kelly, an untenured scientist, and Cathy, an untenured professor of education. I'm not sure why we have two outside members, but I don't ask. I like both Kelly and Cathy very much and am happy to be working with them.

We agreed at our initial meeting in November on the strategy described earlier for winnowing down our list of candidates from the seventy-five or so applications we have: the candidates were divided into five alphabetical ranges, and each of us will read the files of two different ranges and choose our top candidates from those ranges. That way each range will have been read by two different faculty members, and none of us will be overwhelmed. We are to write up brief notes about our candidates of choice, which Kim will photocopy and circulate to all.

We have advertised in two areas: the ad called for either a specialist in eighteenth-century literature or a specialist in writing and communications (courses that are becoming increasingly popular here as on many other campuses). The dual nature of the ad has evoked a strange mix of candidates, from Ivy League theorists in eighteenth-century literature to writing specialists from large state schools.

I have put myself into a somewhat awkward position by encouraging a friend of mine to apply. He and I both earned our Ph.D.'s at Northwestern. He took a position at a Chicago-area community college a year or two after I graduated. He has spoken quite positively about his job at the community college and seems happy there, but his wife wants to move to the East Coast, to be closer to her family, so he has put himself on the market.

Although his Ph.D. work did not focus on either eighteenth-century literature or writing and communications, he has taught more writing classes than anyone I know, has written a book of nonfiction himself, and has an informed understanding of writing theory and practice. He is also one of the most dedicated and thoughtful teachers I know. So I e-mailed him about the job and encouraged him to apply. His name falls into my range, and I select him as one of my top choices. At the first meeting in December I mention that I know him and that I think he would fit in well at Assumption.

Kelly and I both have him on our short lists when we come to the next meeting, to narrow the candidates down to ten or twelve for phone interviews. Then something odd happens. When we come to his name, I mention again that while he doesn't have formal training in writing, I think he has enough practical experience to compensate. But it turns out that his formal education is not the problem.

"I'm sure he's wonderful," Kim says, "but I think we really need to hire someone in eighteenth-century literature. This is the second time we have included the eighteenth century as a possible field in a search—the first was with your search—and I think the department really wants us to hire in that area this time around."

Maurice nods in agreement, and it seems plain to me that they both have known this all along. Why, then, I wonder, did we even bother to advertise in the other area? I suspect there might be something political going on here. Maybe the writing-and-communications part of the ad was a nod or concession to someone—someone obviously not on this committee. Frankly, I'm not sure I want to know. I also don't want to prolong the meeting, so I accept the explanation, and we weed out all candidates who are not specialists in the eighteenth century.

We end up with nine candidates with whom we will conduct telephone interviews. Although the standard practice in English is to conduct preliminary interviews at the Modern Language Association's annual convention, we apparently do not have enough money in our search budget to pay the registration and hotel fees associated with conducting interviews there. I was disconcerted at first to hear this. What kind of college had I joined that couldn't afford to send a few people to MLA? Since then I have learned that more and more schools are following this pattern, according to friends who report having their first interviews conducted by telephone.

Of our nine candidates, only three are men, and one of those three is out of the country and declares himself unavailable for phone interviewing during the break. (How badly does he want a job, I wonder, if he expects both to miss the convention and to be unavailable for phone interviews for a month?) I get the feeling that, as a committee, we are giving especially long looks at the female candidates, although no one says anything explicit about this to me. This may have been another reason why my friend didn't make it to this stage of the process.

I actually have no problem with biasing ourselves towards a female candidate, if in fact that's what we're doing (I will never know for certain). The department's last five hires—Mark and I, Charles, Ed, and Dan— were all male, and of the department's six women, two are within five or ten years of retirement. Combine that with the fact that most of our English majors are women, and it seems to me that we should be trying to hire a woman.

In the second and third weeks of break, we conduct our telephone interviews, in pairs, with eight candidates (the inaccessible applicant has fallen out of the running).

I conduct one interview with Maurice, one with Kim, and two with Cathy. Two candidates impress me, two do not. The one who stands out by far is Rebecca, whom Cathy and I interview. She describes her dissertation—a study of the built environment of seventeenth- and eighteenth-century London, and of how certain theories and ideas manifest themselves in both the literature and the architecture of the period—in such a way that I feel like asking her to mail it right up to me, I'd like to read it. She talks easily and intelligently; she is articulate and has a sense of humor; she speaks passionately about her dissertation research; and she describes teaching practices that indicate to me that she would fit in well here. She has been one of our top choices from the beginning—Maurice wrote "She's the one!" in his notes about her—but now she vaults to the very top of Cathy's and my lists.

Another candidate impresses me. Aaron has his law degree, as well as his Ph.D., and he comes from a prestigious Catholic university and speaks about that in his letter. I am surprised that the committee has not discussed the religious background of any of the candidates, given the Catholic affiliation of the college, but no one has mentioned it once. It seems to me that candidates who self-identify with the Catholic mission of the college—as I did, in my cover letter and interview—would prove a good fit, though, so I have been keeping an eye out for that. Aaron fits that bill, and he also brings something different to the table. His background in law might put him in an excellent position to counsel students interested in law school and coach them through the application process. When Kim and I interview him by phone, he speaks intelligently and fulfills the promise of his letter. He stays on the short list.

One of the candidates who doesn't impress me on the phone, when Cathy and I interview him, is someone whose letter and CV I found very promising. This applicant had described in his letter what struck me as an innovative classroom project he undertakes with his composition students, who put together a magazine over the course of the semester, producing both the writing and the graphics. On the phone, though, he is clearly nervous, and the conversation does not go well. I question him pretty closely on how he teaches a typical class—I do this with all the candidates—and he can't come up with anything much to say beyond that he lectures and holds discussions. I am trying to give him the opportunity to describe one or two really striking things he does in the classroom, but either he doesn't do anything striking or he can't figure out that this is what I'm after. Either way, it doesn't bode well for him, and after the interview he drops off the short list.

We invite Rebecca and Aaron to campus, as well as a third candidate, Kerry, whom I did not interview. Kerry has an assistant professor's position at a university in the Southwest, where she carries a heavy teaching load and is far from her friends and family. Our position would represent steps up in those areas, and apparently she acquitted herself well in the phone interview. I don't find her nearly as impressive as Rebecca on paper. The research projects she describes seem more traditional than Rebecca's, not as imaginative or intellectually challenging. And she has what strikes me as one serious drawback: while she wrote her dissertation in the area of eighteenth-century literature, she is currently working on a research project about a different period in English literature, the Victorian era.

Kerry's campus visit comes first, but unfortunately I have either class or family obligations during her teaching demonstration and her interview with the entire department. I do meet her informally, and she seems personable and at ease during our conversation, which is a good sign. While I wouldn't want to punish a candidate for showing signs of nervousness, these small things do matter. We speak in public for a living and occasionally are called upon to speak formally before groups of our peers or administrators, and the ability to handle such situations with grace and ease seems to me a definite requirement for the job.

Aaron visits on the following day, in the first week of February, and I am able to attend both his interview and his teaching demonstration. Unfortunately, the demonstration does not go well. It goes so badly, in fact, that it dooms his candidacy.

To my mind, he does one thing in the demonstration that is emblematic of what I take to be his approach to teaching. As with the other candidates, we asked him to teach a forty-minute lesson on a subject of his choosing to an audience of English faculty and a handful of our majors. We are in a function room, not a traditional classroom; we have set up a podium at the front of the room, and we are all seated at round tables. Aaron has requested a projector to show some visuals, and he has a handout of excerpts from an eighteenth-century work for us to analyze together—both good ideas. He has also selected an interesting topic, and I look forward to seeing how he will approach our students.

But for the entire forty-five minutes of his presentation, Aaron never once steps out from behind the podium. He smiles and does his best to perform in a relaxed manner, but he seems wooden and uncomfortable. When he asks questions of the students—and to his credit, he does ask them—he very clearly has certain right answers in mind that he expects to hear. The students figure this out quickly, as they always do, and clam up, not wanting to guess wrong.

By the end of the demonstration, Aaron is out of the running as far as I am concerned. I can imagine myself getting very bored, very quickly, if I were a student in his class. I may have unrealistic expectations for the high-pressure situation of a teaching demonstration, but I want to see what I want to see: a professor who really engages the students, who makes an effort to come out into their space and invite them into the lesson. The way his feet seemed glued to the floor, while a small thing, could be symptomatic of a top-down approach to teaching: I have the answers, and you will learn them from me.

The world doesn't need more faculty who think that way about teaching; we have enough of them already. Aaron certainly didn't *say* he thought that way, in either his cover letter or the subsequent interview. He may be a wonderfully innovative teacher, and the artificial situation of the demonstration simply forced him into another mode. But we have no way of verifying that.

Rebecca, God bless her, does everything right. Her teaching demonstration, on Thursday of that same intense week of interviewing, is energetic, makes use of visuals and handouts as well, and engages students in the ways I had hoped to see Aaron doing. She walks out into the middle of the room, approaching students when they contribute, and seems genuinely interested in their responses. She is dynamic, makes a joke or two, and I find myself caught up in her subject matter, wanting to participate in the discussion. All excellent signs.

After she has concluded, we give her a short break, and then we gather around three tables and everyone in the department has the opportunity to ask her questions. I remember from my own interview how exhausted I was at this stage, so exhausted, in fact, that I didn't have the energy to be nervous. This probably helped my performance. Rebecca seems to be in a similar state of exhaustion, but she handles herself well.

Dan, our poet, asks her the same question he asked me, and which he apparently asks every job candidate we have: "Can you recite for me a piece of literature you have memorized?"

It seemed like a completely bizarre question when he asked it of me last year, not to mention one I wouldn't have anticipated in a million years. But of course I didn't want to say or imply that, so I did my best and stretched my memory for the first stanza of a Philip Larkin poem. Rebecca is more honest than I was, or perhaps just more exhausted: "I don't really memorize very well," she says simply, and deflects the question.

Whatever the reason she did it, I admire her all the more for the answer. I understand Dan's intention—at a college this small, we are all required to teach general-education courses in literature, and he is testing our candidates' commitment to literature and the word—but the question still strikes me as a strange one, and I hope she isn't put off by it. By the time the interview ends, I am already starting to think about how to recruit her.

I have the opportunity to begin that recruitment a few minutes after the end of the interview, since I will be driving her to the restaurant for her final stop of the day, dinner with four of us from the department. I escort her to the Lang family mini-van—hastily cleared that morning of scattered juice boxes, crushed goldfish crackers, empty water bottles and Diet Coke cans, CD cases and oil-change receipts—and we set off on the fifteen-minute drive across town to an expensive Italian restaurant.

"So listen," I say, after a few minutes of polite conversation, "this is your one opportunity to find out anything you want to know about this job or the department or the college. I'm only in my first year here, I just went through this all myself a year ago, and I promise to be perfectly honest with you about anything you want to know."

She doesn't ask me anything too difficult at first, just general questions about the position that anyone in the department could answer. Finally, though, she takes me up on my offer.

"Are you happy here?"

"I am," I say, and I'm glad she has asked this. "I feel very comfortable here, and I could probably spend the rest of my life at this college."

It feels true as I say it, which is a revelation to me. Despite all the difficulties with my teaching, I am confident that I can eventually turn my fortunes in the classroom around. I am comfortable with the college's religious affiliation, which matches my own. I have made good friendships with Mark and Ed and Dan, and Anne has just been offered a full-time job as a long-term sub for the rest of the year in a school that backs up to the Assumption campus. She is hopeful that she may be hired there permanently next year. Things seem to be falling into place for me at the college, and for us in our private lives as well.

Rebecca and I are at the restaurant by the time we get to that question, and as we walk from the street to the door I extend the offer of truthful answers by encouraging her to e-mail me if any other question occurs to her. Then we are seated at the table, where Rebecca does the one final thing that seals the deal for me: she orders a beer.

Now that's the kind of candidate I can really get behind. (Of course, she orders only one.)

Back at home that evening, with only two viable candidates remaining, as far as I'm concerned, and with all the talk I've heard and the papers I've read about the eighteenth century running together in my mind, I go back to thinking about the candidates as people.

Kerry struck me as open, sincere, warm, and personable. She seemed like someone who would get along well with the people in our department. Rebecca, on the other hand, seemed a little distant, reluctant to say anything beyond what a job candidate might be expected to say. It is difficult to gauge her personality, and that could come back to haunt us if we hire her and find that personality to be not congenial. But from her writing and teaching demonstration, I can tell that Rebecca is whip-smart. She might not fit in easily, but she would bring something new, exciting, and invigorating to the department. Kerry might prove to be the more friendly colleague, but we're not hiring someone for customer service; intellectual challenge is what it's all about. I want the brains, and by the time I go to bed, my mind is made up.

That Friday afternoon we all gather around a squared group of tables, with an open space in the middle. We are not in our usual cramped meeting room. For some reason we are meeting in the function room in which we watched the candidates' teaching demonstrations, a setting that gives the meeting a distinctly formal air. Drinks, fruit, and cheese have been set out on a table in one corner, and as people chat and choose their seats, they pile food onto small plates and fill cups with coffee or tea.

The chair opens the meeting by announcing the format. Each of us will be given the opportunity to make a pitch for our candidate of choice. We will go around the table in the order we are seated. Once we have all said our piece, we will vote on the candidate by secret ballot. A simple majority will decide the vote.

From conversations in the hallway over the past day or two, I can tell that we are really debating only two candidates: Kerry and Rebecca. Aaron has dropped from most people's short lists and has become an almost-unanimous third choice. In the speeches that follow, most people acknowledge that Aaron would probably do just fine, but that he stands a cut below our top two choices.

I am sitting at a corner of the table to the left of the chair, and I speak first. I am at a slight disadvantage in that I didn't see Kerry's teaching demonstration and so can't make a point-by-point comparison of the two candidates. I decide to focus on the positive things I saw in Rebecca's demonstration.

"I guess I would evaluate the two of them in four categories," I say. "Research, teaching, service, and how well I think they would fit into the department.

"They have similar service records, and I think they would fit equally well into the department, so those categories are a wash. When I conducted the phone interview with Rebecca, I was extremely impressed by her research. She seems to be doing something really innovative and interesting, something that could add to the course offerings of the department. It's not that Kerry's research is substandard; it's just that Rebecca's seems superior.

"I know that we're not a research school, and that the likelihood of Rebecca's turning her dissertation into a book is not the most important consideration here. But conceiving of such a dissertation topic and then carrying it through—that strikes me as comparable to conceiving of a new course or a new service project. It requires the same level of imagination, intellectual ability, and discipline. The fact that she came up with this topic and then pursued it suggests to me that she has the better mind for this job—that she will be capable of coming up with equally exciting new course offerings or new ideas for the college.

"I didn't see both candidates teach, so I can't really compare them on that score. But I read what they both had to say about teaching, I spoke with them both about it, and I can analyze what I saw with Rebecca." Here I pull out what I think of as my trump card. "When I was at the Searle Center, we were conducting a long-term study of the habits of the most highly effective college teachers. And I can assure you, as I watched Rebecca and heard her talk about her teaching, that she exhibited almost every one of the characteristics that we saw in those outstanding teachers."

I mention some of the details of her teaching demonstration—her energy and enthusiasm, her use of mixed media (she also had slides and printed excerpts for us to consider), her stepping out from behind the podium and engaging the students directly, her ability to work with what the students gave her rather than trying to lead them to say what she wanted to hear—and note the sound pedagogical principles underlying those techniques.

"So in two categories I see them as even," I conclude, "but in both teaching and research I would give the nod to Rebecca."

Charles is sitting next to me, and, true to his generally contrarian nature, he begins by undercutting what I had thought was my most convincing point.

"Well, I did see Kerry teach," he says, not looking at me, "and I can tell you that every one of those points Jim just ran down, which demonstrated what a great teacher Rebecca was, Kerry did as well. So if that's how you are going to evaluate them, then don't be swayed by his speech to vote for Rebecca. They both had those same teaching qualities."

The remark surprises me. Charles's own publication record suggests that he values research over teaching, and I would have expected him to support the candidate with the more promising record in that area. I also feel a flush of anxiety. Is he criticizing me for having missed Kerry's teaching demonstration? I suddenly feel self-conscious about this, even though I know I am not the only one who missed one of the teaching demos. I settle back into my chair and wait for him to speak in defense of Kerry.

But Charles's speech is not what I expect. In fact, by the end of his two minutes, I can't tell which candidate he supports. He lists positives and negatives for both and then just stops. He doesn't conclude with any sort of definitive statement for or against either candidate.

A similar speech follows from one of the senior professors in the department. He analyzes the candidates as he saw them, includes some positive and negative comments about each, then stops. He seems to lean towards Kerry, but only slightly. Did I make some sort of mistake in arguing for my candidate? Are we supposed to remain neutral in our speeches and then express our opinion through the vote?

But no. The next few speeches clearly express an opinion, and they express it for Kerry. A point that begins to recur in the speeches in favor of Kerry is her ability to fit into the department.

"I want to make sure we hire someone who will be here with us in another ten or fifteen years," says one senior faculty member. "I thought Rebecca was wonderful too, but I am not sure we are the right school for her. I think Kerry is the sort of person who could spend her entire career here."

Even if Rebecca stayed here for only two or three years, I think to myself, we would be a better department for it. I am willing to take the chance on the better candidate and hope that she can push us in new directions during her time here, however short it may be. But the tide of the discussion has definitely turned in favor of Kerry, and I sense that the vote is headed in that direction, too. After my push for Rebecca, most of the speakers have either been neutral or have favored Kerry.

But four speakers remain before we get to the chair, and now the tide rolls back Rebecca's way.

The last speaker is Kelly, the scientist who served as one of the outside members of the search committee. One of the speakers for Rebecca had articulated a version of what I had just been thinking: that Rebecca would bring something new to the department, even if that something might not seem at first to be a perfect fit. Kelly picks up on this point and makes an argument based on the importance of hiring for diversity.

"There are lots of different kinds of diversity," she says. "We talk about the importance of diversity all the time, and here we have the opportunity to hire someone who is not just like all of us—or like many of us. True, Rebecca might not seem like the most comfortable fit for what we have here now, but that might be a good thing. I think she can challenge us. I think she will bring a diversity we need here at the college."

The chair now calls for volunteers to coordinate the secret vote. I'm surprised that there is going to be no actual debate, no chance to respond to other people's comments, but someone else needs this room at 7 P.M., and the hour is approaching.

We vote. Rebecca wins.

The chair announces that she will call to make an offer immediately, then closes the meeting.

The meeting had its moments of tension. Some of the later speakers referred obliquely—and sometimes not so obliquely—to comments that had preceded theirs, and somehow this felt awkward, since earlier speakers did not have the opportunity to respond to later ones. The meeting's adjournment is businesslike, and people are cordial but not especially chatty as they pack their bags, grab a leftover cookie or bottle of water, and move to the door. We clear out of the room singly or in pairs. Mark and I go back to our offices, and in the hallway we cautiously sound one another out on the different arguments we heard, and on the arguments we seemed to be hearing underneath the spoken ones.

After the meeting, I think about the speeches, about conversations I have had with other faculty about the candidates, and also about more general conversations I have had with them. Faintly, like slowly clarifying lines drawn with invisible ink, the lines separating the two major factions in the department start to emerge.

A small group of people offered pretty similar speeches in favor of Kerry and kept coming back to the notions of collegiality and fit. They clearly preferred the candidate who looks more like themselves than the one who would bring something new to the department. They strike me as faculty who have settled comfortably into their roles as teachers, who do that part of their jobs well, and who would prefer that the college maintain its current emphasis on teaching over publication.

As someone who would like to see the college reduce teaching loads in favor of stepped-up expectations for publishing, I would like to see us hiring more people who share that outlook and who offer the promise of productive scholarly careers. As a newcomer, I have no set vision of the college influencing my perspective, and no doubt I see it as more malleable than my senior colleagues might. Like all new hires, I have come in and want to remake the faculty in my own image. I would love to see a faculty of researchers and writers, people with whom I could collaborate and share the joys and frustrations of writing and publishing.

Others in the department must share my vision as well—or perhaps they saw something else in Rebecca that made them vote for her. But I think I have discovered the key to the alliances and divisions among my colleagues: it is their different perspectives on the college's emphasis on teaching over research. For a long time after that meeting, I will believe that this is the primary factor determining departmental alliances. It will take me several years to see that it is only one of many factors, ranging in seriousness from beliefs about the shape of the department to personal squabbles.

Not everyone in the department falls into one of the two camps I have begun to identify. Maurice's status as the department's elder statesman and his evident genuine goodwill keep him out of these battles. No one ever has a bad word to say about him, and he says a bad word about nobody. Dan cultivates a studied neutrality, at least in my presence. I have no idea whom he likes or doesn't like, whom he allies with or whom he distrusts. Charles too never tips his hand. He seems focused on his own work and expresses little interest, to me or in public, in the larger arguments swirling around the department or the college. He keeps his head down and his mouth shut. His carefully neutral speech at the meeting struck me as emblematic of his larger attitude.

In the end, I came to see our hiring of this candidate as I now believe you have to see the hiring of all candidates: as a struggle for the soul of the department. When you vote for a candidate, you vote for a specific vision of the department, and that vision can often be hotly contested. It clearly was in our case, as we cast our votes for either a department that would continue to replicate its current values or one that would head in a new direction, the endpoint of which was not entirely clear.

Some of my colleagues obviously saw that uncertain future as frightening and unwelcome. For me it meant challenge, excitement, and movement towards the sort of department and college in which I could happily spend my career.

I make one last personal attempt to sway Rebecca, and the following week, after the offer has been tendered, I send her an e-mail saying simply that I hope she will join us, and that I will be happy to answer any remaining questions she might have, in the same candid spirit as our discussion in the car.

Her response is friendly but noncommittal, and I leave it at that. Given her interview skills and her strengths as a candidate, I am sure that she has other interviews, perhaps even other offers. I wonder how we stack up against her other opportunities.

One week after we make her the offer, she accepts.

It feels like a victory to me, and I wonder whether I have taken a permanent side in what may prove to be an ongoing battle for the soul of the department. Do I really want to be taking sides during my first year on the tenure track? At the meeting, should I have just kept my mouth shut, or given one of those neutral speeches, and then quietly voted for Rebecca? Will the senior faculty member who spoke for Kerry, and those who shared her perspective, begin to regard me in a different light, as a potential antagonist in departmental discussions?

That anxiety dissipates the following week when one of those senior faculty members makes a point of stopping by my office and chatting in a friendly way, assuring me that she thinks Rebecca will be a wonderful colleague. We make some plans for an upcoming event we are helping to coordinate, and I feel absolutely no tension or distrust from her.

So while I have definitely taken a side in this particular battle, it doesn't feel as though I have committed myself to anything I can't change in the future. I can see that the department has its divisions, but all departments do, and in the week or two following the meeting they seem to recede in the face of midterms and the obligations of the spring semester.

What finally knocks them fully out of my consciousness, at least for a month or two, is the one thing I have been doing my best to ignore: my health. A week in the hospital, as I will learn at the end of February, does wonders for your perspective on the significance of battles for the soul of the department.

Living

The spring semester brings me three entirely new course preparations, four classes, and around eighty students. Not all of those students are new. In fact, I am gratified to see at least a dozen of my former composition students in my two sections of Introduction to Literature—further proof to me that the semester couldn't possibly have gone as badly as it felt while I was living through it.

Some students I am happy to have back, like Ben, whose Red Sox cap—and willingness to participate in class discussions—will be joining me for another semester. Another student I'm happy to see is Jamie, the musician who wrote one of the best papers of the semester, an essay about the lyrics of a song by the rock group Live. Jamie talks in class, and I am discovering that, while of course I welcome the really smart students, even when they are quiet—like Margaret, the outstanding writer from the British fiction class—I welcome even more those students whom I can count on to contribute intelligently and consistently in class.

I am a little distressed, therefore, to see a few students who clearly were not comfortable speaking in class last semester. Mary, the student who did her best to hide her tall frame from me for the entire semester, and whose limited writing skills proved to be one of the most difficult challenges to my pedagogical skills, sauntered into class on the first day of the new semester, didn't look at me or acknowledge me, and went right to the back row. Since I obviously didn't spark her intellectual interest in composition, all I can imagine is that the devil she knows apparently beats the devil she doesn't—or that my sections were the only ones scheduled for a time slot when she could take Introduction to Literature, a general-education requirement for all students.

I have twenty-six and twenty-seven students in the two different sections. The cap is twenty-five, but I wasn't able to resist signing in a few composition students who came to me begging to get into the course. I wanted to say no, because I knew that each extra student would add five or ten hours of work for me over the next four months in the form of grading quizzes and papers. In the future I will do this less and less. Dan makes the point to me later in the semester that if the administration sees us consistently letting in students over the enrollment cap, they may raise those enrollment caps, meaning more students for all of us every semester.

I also have twenty students in a course called Argument and Persuasion, which is an intermediate composition course required for a couple of different majors. And I am teaching an upper-level class in postcolonial literature, in which we are reading texts by and about writers from England's former colonies. That class has only eight students, two of whom are also in Argument and Persuasion. I haven't taught either of these students before, and it seems bizarre to me that they would elect for two courses with a professor they don't know. They are going to have had their fill of Professor Lang by the end of the semester.

I have taken on one other teaching responsibility as well. With my budding interest in writing creative nonfiction, I proposed to the chair during the fall semester the possibility that I might teach an advanced writing workshop in the genre. She was interested in the idea but told me I would have to write a proposal for the course, which would then have to pass the curriculum committee. She gave me the proposal guidelines, which were pretty extensive: I needed a syllabus, a list of possible texts, a bibliography of relevant works in the field, and written responses to a series of questions about how the course would fit into the current curriculum.

I worked on it over break and submitted it to the committee in early February. But since everyone knew I was working on this proposal—I had to clear it with the department in a meeting at the end of the fall semester—a colleague has already sent me a student who was looking for an independent study in this kind of writing. Since I had just begun to think about the shape of the course when the student came to me, in early December, I agreed to work with him. I thought my experience with him would help prepare me for the course, which I would have the opportunity to teach in the fall semester of the following year.

So he and I are meeting for an hour once a week—I schedule it during my office hours, which I'm not sure is condoned—and we have laid out a series of readings and assignments for him to do in creative nonfiction writing.

To my happy surprise, all four classes have been going well from the start—a marked improvement from last semester. Since so many of the students in Introduction to Literature already know me—and some of them got friends to sign up for the course, too—they know what to expect, and the participation levels in the discussions are high. I feel comfortable with the students and often will walk around before class making chitchat. I also decide to shock those students out of their complacency, and establish the tenor of the class, at the very beginning of the semester.

On the first day of class, I read them two poems: Dylan Thomas's "Do Not Go Gentle into That Good Night," which is a villanelle—a traditional poem with a formal rhyme and metrical pattern—and Philip Larkin's "This Be the Verse," which begins like this:

> They fuck you up, your mum and dad.
> They may not mean to, but they do.
> They fill you with the faults they had
> And add some extra, just for you.

I could see jaws dropping when I said the word "fuck"—and I stressed it, as the rhythm of the poem demands. Afterwards, to introduce them to the concept of literary genres and the role our expectations play in shaping those genres, I had them write a short paragraph about which of the two poems sounded to them more like their idea of a poem, and I asked a dozen of them to share their responses with the class. I talked with them about how their preconceptions about poetry shape their poetry-reading experience, and about how artists sometimes deliberately break the rules of their genre in order to grab the reader's attention or to make a point. That exercise seemed to loosen the students up a bit, and to establish from the very outset that this would be an interesting class—and that they were expected to help make it interesting.

In Argument and Persuasion the students are junior and senior communications majors. They too are very talkative, but I also did something there to help. I had them fill out the standard information sheets on the first day, as I always do. When they handed them in to me, I pulled up my chair in front of the desk and sat down, casually crossing one leg over the other.

"What I'm about to do is not designed to embarrass anyone or put them on the spot," I said. "But we are going to be arguing with one another all semester, and I want us to feel comfortable with one another, and I want you to feel comfortable with me. This will help us get to that place."

I then took the top sheet, which told me that Matt was a communications major, found Matt, and asked, "So, Matt, what do you want to do with your life?"

Matt was clearly taken aback, not expecting that question, but I kept my tone light and joked with him a bit about his uncertain future. He responded well, laughing and seeming to enjoy the class's momentary attention on him.

After Matt, I went through the information sheets one by one, talking for a minute or two with each student. I asked them about their major, their career plans, or what they did over the summer. I made jokes and tried to keep everything as informal as possible. It seems to have worked: it humanized me in their eyes, familiarized them with one another, and broke the opening-day tension. The students in that class are now participating happily.

The same has been true of the small postcolonial-literature class, in part just because it's a small class. Most of them know each other already, and two of them I also see in Argument and Persuasion, so the discussions there are moving along as well.

By mid-February I feel that I have the courses in good rhythms, and the classroom sessions are going well. I am enjoying the chance to see some of my repeat students and to track their progress. I also just feel more comfortable in the classroom, slightly less anxious about the possibility that things will go horribly wrong. That comfort level allows me to relax in the classroom, to joke around a little bit, and to banter more easily with the students.

In that first paper in Introduction to Literature, a good dozen of the students said that their purpose in reading a poem was to discover the poem's "hidden meaning." I don't like that phrase, which suggests that poems are like crossword puzzles or acrostics, and that poets deliberately hide their meanings from us. So on the day I handed back their first papers, I delivered a mini-lecture on the problems with that concept of reading poetry and told them to avoid that phrase in future papers.

The next class period, I was talking about the plan for the day and fumbling around in those opening moments of class when I have to get myself into the rhythm of the period, which takes a few minutes. "So by the end of the class we are going to get at this story's . . . ," and then I paused, momentarily unable to recall the word I wanted, which was "theme."

Jamie took advantage of that pause. "Hidden meaning?" he asked loudly.

The class burst into laughter, and I had to laugh myself—it was clever and funny.

"That's enough out of you for the day, hidden-meaning boy," I said to him, falling into rhythm at that moment. "Theme is what I meant to say. So let's get started."

But in that moment, and in that called-out joke, I was ecstatic to see that I had created in this classroom the sort of atmosphere I strove for last semester, one in which we can work seriously but in which students also feel comfortable bantering with me and with each other.

But the classroom is pretty much the only place things are going well. I am finding the three different course preparations—again, all new—and the grading of papers for eighty students almost impossible to manage. I feel as if I am always one task behind where I should be on my list of things to do. I finish my course preparations for one day, then suddenly I have a new stack of papers to grade and a *Chronicle* column to write. I get through grading a stack of papers, and now I have two new course preps and a departmental meeting, and I have to respond to five e-mails from students. On top of those regular responsibilities, I am supposed to be going to a conference at the end of February, to give a paper based on that abstract I turned in late in October, and I still haven't written the paper. In the first two weeks of February we have our candidate interviews, and then the long meeting for the vote, all of which takes up additional time I can't afford to give.

And as if all that weren't enough, I'm still sick.

I will fully realize this only in retrospect, when I start to get better in the late spring, but I have been sick all year. You get used to anything eventually, and I have been sick for so long now that I hardly even think of it as being sick anymore. There hasn't been a single day in three months when I've been in the bathroom fewer than a half-dozen times. I occasionally see blood in the toilet, which indicates persistent inflammation and hemorrhaging in my intestinal tract. This leaves me anemic and creates a constant low-grade fatigue. I started a new medication in January, one that has worked wonders for many Crohn's patients, but it can take as long as six months to start to work, so it won't be bailing me out anytime soon. I'd probably be depressed if I had the time to think about it, but I've just barely got my nostrils above the waterline, and the furious and constant treading of water keeps me distracted.

Everything comes crashing down on the evening of Monday, February 12. I come home from school in the late afternoon, having taught my two classes for that day in the morning and stayed at school to grade papers for the remainder of the day. Anne isn't home. She has taken the girls somewhere and left me a note saying that she won't be home until after dinner.

I'm too tired to make dinner. I find a couple of pieces of leftover bacon in the fridge—not the ideal source of nutrition for someone with an inflamed intestinal tract, but I'm too exhausted to care—and start munching on them as I search around for something easy and filling to eat. But before I can find anything, a powerful wave of nausea overwhelms me, and I run to the bathroom to vomit. I'm in there again another half-dozen times over the next few hours. Crohn's is an autoimmune disorder, which means that when the immune system becomes active for some other reason—like to fight the flu I've obviously just come down with—it can trigger disease activity. So of course my Crohn's immediately flares up with a vengeance, and I have it coming out both ends so persistently that by 11 P.M. I can tell that I am becoming dangerously dehydrated, and that I may not be able to stop vomiting until I can find an alternative way—not through the stomach—to get rehydrated.

So we call a neighbor to sit with the kids, and Anne drops me off at the emergency room. I am there all night, on IV hydration, and am feeling a little better by the time dawn appears in a window that I can just glimpse through a crack in the curtains that surround my bed. Anne picks me up early in the morning, before her school, and I rest at home that day. But the diarrhea and vomiting don't stop and in fact are getting worse. Two days later I am in the hospital again for another night of IV hydration. I come back home again the next morning, but two days after that I am admitted for a six-day stay, during which I will be receiving intense dosages of one of my regular medications in IV form.

I returned home from the hospital, after that first night in the emergency room, on a Tuesday morning, which was not a class day for me. I e-mailed the department secretary and canceled my office hours for the day. The next morning I called her and asked her to cancel my classes. On Thursday, after my second night in the emergency room, I had her cancel Friday's classes as well.

On Saturday, when I had settled into my hospital bed for the first afternoon of my six-day stay, with my laptop and school bag at my bedside, I tried to figure out how to cover a week's worth of classes without me being there. Of course I should have been resting, but the drug I was taking was prednisone, which has sleeplessness as one of its many unpleasant side effects. And I had a pressing reason for feeling that I had to cover my classes: we simply could not afford for me to go on sick leave for the rest of the semester. Somehow, despite the week I had already missed and the next week I was bound to miss, I had to keep my classes functioning and under my control.

With the help of my friends and my wife, I managed it, though just barely. After the success of my experiments with music last semester, I had incorporated it into the syllabus for Introduction to Literature this semester. We were spending five weeks talking about poetry, at the end of which we were to spend a couple of classes talking about the poetry of rock lyrics. I had then set aside a week of classes for students to offer presentations to the class, in pairs, playing part of a rock song and interpreting its lyrics using the poetic terms to which I had introduced them in the previous five weeks.

I had missed the two classes in which we were going to analyze lyrics together, but I was confident that they could still manage the presentations. By a happy coincidence, the week I spent in the hospital was Anne's spring break. So I sent her into class with a video camera, and she taped my students' presentations and brought the tapes home so that I could watch them and grade them after I returned from the hospital. She wasn't able to adjust completely from elementary school to college teaching; on one occasion, when a couple of students were talking in the back of the room, she put her finger to her lips and shushed them.

(I've never been a shush-er. At the Searle Center we had an acting teacher who would give workshops about how to manipulate classroom space for pedagogical effect, and she taught me a good trick to help silence unruly students. When students are talking in class, I continue whatever I am doing—talking, listening, reading aloud—and walk to their desks and stand right behind or next to them. My immediate presence almost always silences the talkers, and they are usually savvy enough to recognize it as a rebuke.)

By another happy coincidence, I had scheduled a movie for the postcolonial-literature class during the upcoming week. I asked Mark to show up in class and play the movie for me, which he did. He collected some short papers and dropped them off for me when I was back home.

In Argument and Persuasion, I had regular classes scheduled, so on Saturday in the hospital I typed up a long explanation of what I had planned and asked help from anyone who might be able to step in and cover the material for me for a class or two. I minimized the lesson plans and assured my would-be helpers that they did not need to hold a full class. I saved the message on a disk and had Mark send it around in an e-mail message to the department. Laura picked up one class, and Ed the other one. So I managed to keep that class covered as well.

On Thursday of the following week I am released from the hospital, starting to feel better. I have a fistful of new prescription bottles to see me through the next few months of recovery. I have lost a good twenty-five pounds and am so weak that I have to catch my breath after walking up the stairs to my bedroom. My mother has flown in from Cleveland to help Anne take care of the girls, and with the two of them working together I am able to rest and recover for a few days.

As insane as it seems to the two of them and to my doctor—and even, in my saner moments, to me—I am determined to return to class on Monday. Spring break is only one week off, so I will have to soldier through just one week of classes before getting some time off. I have already withdrawn from the conference I was supposed to attend, so I will have no obligations except for grading during that break week.

If I were to analyze my motivations, I would realize that professional insecurity is what is pushing me back into the classroom so quickly. I don't want to prove a burden to my colleagues. I know that if a colleague were to ask me to cover his classes, in the semester I have been having, either I would say no or I would say yes and resent it. I imagine others must feel the same way. It never occurs to me that my late-junior and senior colleagues might have their lives under better control than I do, in my first year, and that such a request might not present the challenge for them that it would for me.

I don't want my students to take my illness too seriously, and I don't much feel like talking to them about it, but its effects are clearly visible in my frame. I offer a nonspecific explanation at the beginning of each class, attributing my illness to a virus—which is partially true. They laugh and look a little incredulous when I show them the pillow I have brought to class and explain that I need to put it on my chair because I no longer have any fat in my butt, which makes sitting on hard chairs a painful experience.

I have papers and presentations to grade and return in all classes, and I ask for their patience. It is one of the few times in my teaching career when it takes me longer than a week to turn around student work. I explain that I will have all work back to them the first class after spring break, but I need the time until then.

(My habit of turning student work around quickly is a point that students always note in my favor on their evaluations of me. It sounds like a small issue, but it apparently matters a good deal to them. The practice also has pedagogical implications. The sooner students get their work back, the more likely they are to make changes to their writing.)

I make it through the week by doing no grading and using as many interactive exercises as possible in class. I tell the students I really need their help in contributing that week, because I just don't have the strength to do it all myself, and they oblige.

In the fall semester I had bought a used recliner from the Salvation Army for my office, and on my first day back at school I bring an alarm clock. After classes I recline in my chair and take short naps, or just close my eyes and rest.

Outside my office and my classroom, the department hums along without me, and occasionally I wonder if there has been any fallout from the hiring meeting. But mostly I remain deliberately oblivious to the rest of the department. I really have no intellectual or emotional energy to spare right now, and it's best for me to keep to myself and fulfill my obligations to my students. My responsibilities on the hiring committee have obviously come to a close, and I have no other pressing service obligations.

My week in the hospital and those weeks away from school provide me with the sort of perspective that unfortunately tends to come only with tragedy: illness in the family, the death of loved ones, national tragedies.

In the days that I spend at home during spring break, grading papers and resting as much as possible, I look back over the last six months and see that I have been letting life outside of my job slowly slip from my grasp. I have been ignoring or downplaying the obvious warning signs that my illness had been sending me all year; I haven't seen a dentist since we arrived; I haven't changed the oil in the cars or balanced the checkbook. I have stopped doing the laundry. I never make the bed. I steal as much time away from my children as possible, occasionally asking Anne to let me work in the afternoons while the children are around. We took a weekend trip to Block Island, off the Rhode Island coast, in the early weeks of September, but haven't been anywhere since. Except for my *Chronicle* columns, I haven't written a single word of anything—scholarship or creative nonfiction—since the first day of the semester.

Worst, for me, is the feeling that I have been losing touch with my two daughters. That feeling was intensified by my stay in the hospital, during which six days I saw them only one time—hospital rooms with invalid fathers not being the most friendly places for small children.

When I did return home, Madeleine had already become unused to me. She refused to allow me to help her dress or to prepare her food, and she seemed more tolerant than welcoming of my hugs and my feeble efforts to play with her. I felt awful about it, but I knew I couldn't force myself back into her life. She was too willful for that, too much of a two-year-old.

Katie, the five-year-old, reacted entirely differently, though in a way that brought me equal sorrow. She began to cling to me, frightened by the realization that I could so easily be taken away from her. Shortly after I came home from the hospital, Anne talked to Katie's teacher at a district-wide in-service day. The teacher said that Katie had been complaining of stomachaches the week I returned from the hospital. The teacher knew about my situation and decided to keep her at school unless she exhibited some serious symptoms. When that tactic didn't work, Katie tried a more direct route and simply asked to go home. "I miss my Daddy," she said, and began to cry.

I cried a little bit myself when I heard this story, because I knew that it might happen again and I could do nothing to prevent it. But Katie's reaction underscored and forced me to accept something I had begun to suspect long before I lay down in the bed of that ambulance, IV drip poking into the back of my wrist, on a Tuesday evening in early February: I am letting my life slip away from me. I have allowed the tenure track to become a parasite, permanently attached to me, gnawing away at the parts of myself that I have always valued the most and that I don't want to lose: being a writer, being a father, being a husband, being the sort of person who takes the time to read novels, to watch baseball games, to take his daughters on a hike to the park or to rent a stupid comedy and laugh at it with his wife. Like any good parasite, the tenure track knows that it mustn't be too greedy. It wants me around, it *needs* me around to teach my classes and serve on committees, so it takes away as much of my life as it can, but never so much that I would think to complain about my working conditions or throw up my hands in frustration and walk away.

And I have allowed it to become that parasite—I understand this on some level. I have been doing too much, working too hard, taking on too many new commitments. The part of my brain in which I think about my classes and my work has been slowly ballooning over the first weeks of the spring semester, and I have passively watched it crowd the other parts of my life into smaller and smaller spaces.

That it took a week in the hospital to make me see this with clarity is a reflection of my own stubbornness and sometimes obsessive work ethic. But I do come to see it.

When I arrive in the hospital for the third time, for my week's stay, I bring my laptop and a bag full of papers to grade and books to read for my classes. During the first few days I look at them every once in a while from my hospital bed, then eventually I pick up Arthur Golden's *Memoirs of a Geisha*, a four-hundred-page novel that Anne read recently and enjoyed. It's a book I will probably never teach, and that is therefore of no value to my academic career, but I read the entire thing before I am released, and I just love it.

Back at home, as the weeks pass and I very slowly regain my strength and weight—a process that will continue through the summer—I pull myself back, if not from my actual responsibilities, from the emotional and mental commitment I have made to those responsibilities. I walk into my Introduction to Literature class a few times without a detailed and fully mapped out plan for the discussion, and wing it. Once it fails miserably; once it proves to be the most interesting discussion of the semester. I miss a departmental meeting because I'm just too tired at the end of the day, and I enjoy the extra hour I have at home. I stop wondering so much about the cross- and undercurrents of departmental intrigue and just try to take everything at face value.

These tactics won't work forever—and in another month a contentious meeting will pull us all back into the vicious cycle of departmental politics—but they help me survive the rest of the semester, and the rest of my first year on the tenure track.

I do work hard at one thing in the weeks and months of my recovery: becoming part of my children's lives again. Madeleine, nearly three years old, has become fascinated by art projects—anything with crayons, markers, scissors, and glue. I slowly make my way back into her affections by taking time in the afternoons to sit down and help her glue acorns to paper, cut shapes from construction paper, and scribble in coloring books.

Katie, now five and obviously aware of the possibility that her father can be taken away from her, takes to holding my hand when I walk her home from school. Sometimes I let her hand go when we are jostling our way through a crowd of her back-packed compatriots, but a minute or two later I will feel her small fingers intertwining with mine as she gently pulls me up the hill towards home.

That hand, its quiet but insistent presence, will remind me in those remaining months of the semester that I have a life apart from my illness, as well as a life off the tenure track.

When I sat down to lay out the different topics for this book, I wondered whether I had any useful advice to offer in this particular area, since my experience seemed such an isolated one. How many of my readers would be struggling with Crohn's disease during their first year on the tenure track? And then, during the weeks I spent drafting this very chapter, in the fall of 2003, another terrible thing happened in my life: my mother, who had successfully fought off cancer of the mouth and lymph nodes ten years earlier, learned that her cancer had returned and that it was terminal.

From October through the first week of December I shuttled back and forth from Worcester to Cleveland every other weekend, sometimes by myself, sometimes with just one child, sometimes with the whole family. I made my last trip on the day classes ended, a Wednesday, when my father called to tell me that her time was coming. I had an open-microphone literary reading scheduled the next day, one I had arranged with the student literary magazine I advise, but I talked to Ed and another colleague, and they were happy to take the responsibility for it off my hands, so I didn't hesitate to leave. My mother died that Sunday.

I got back to school, exhausted and shell-shocked, the next Thursday, the next-to-last day of finals week, with sixty final papers to grade, and final grades to calculate, in just four days.

It occurred to me then that while my specific experience of illness was probably unlikely to resonate with many of my readers, the more general experience of having to cope with trauma, illness, or even death in the first year—or first few years—on the tenure track was likely a common one. Even positive experiences, like the birth of a child, can have a powerful and distracting impact on a new faculty member.

Having to work my way through such an ordeal for the second time in four years helped me understand that I did, in fact, have some advice I wanted to convey—one general principle, and one specific suggestion—to anyone who gets knocked backwards a bit on the first-year journey, either by some life-changing event or simply by the overwhelming nature of the experience.

The general principle is a simple one: the world will go on spinning without you for a little bit. Although this sounds obvious, at first blush it may appear otherwise. Your classes, after all, will not go on without you. Some committees may not be able to run without you. And while conference papers and submission deadlines do come and go without you, you may feel that your career will not go on without you meeting those kinds of obligations.

But the college, I have learned, finds ways of operating without any of us. That awareness may bruise an inflated ego—like the one I sometimes have—but it helps when you are confronting a crisis. Don't be afraid to ask for help, and remember that not everyone's experience of the academic year matches your own in your first year on the tenure track. During my first year, I would have been hard-pressed to help out a colleague in trouble; now, in my fourth year, I would see it as far less burdensome and would welcome the opportunity to help out a first-year colleague. I also recognize now that everyone needs help occasionally, and pitching in to help a colleague here and there comes with the territory. No one will survive a forty-year career without confronting personal tragedies and distractions, and without sometimes having to rely on friends and colleagues for help.

I was in the room with my mother, sitting next to her and reading, on that Sunday evening she died. I heard her breathing become labored and saw her face lose its color and her eyelids suddenly roll open. I called in my father and my siblings from the next room, and we were all standing around her, holding hands and praying, as she took her final breath.

Our presence together at the moment of her death was the one positive element in the whole awful experience, and it wouldn't have happened if I had hesitated when my father called me four days earlier and told me that her time was coming. You experience the death of your mother only once, and you are bound to wonder whether you handled every aspect of it as you should have. The one thing I knew I did right was to hand off my responsibilities, leave school behind, and come home when I was called.

The specific suggestion is equally simple: sometime during your first year, whether you need to or not, get up one morning and cancel a day's worth of classes. Make it a day that the semester doesn't hinge upon, of course, but don't think too far in advance about which day it should be.

I make this recommendation, over the protests I can already hear from my readers in the administration, because remembering to live your life off the tenure track requires the occasional mental checkout day. You may be forced into one of those days by a personal tragedy; if you aren't, you need to take one on your own. Those mental checkout days can perform wonders in terms of realigning your perspective, reminding you of what matters to you, and even helping you to remember what you love about the profession.

So don't spend that day off preparing for the next day's classes. Go to the beach. Sit at home and watch soap operas in your pajamas. If you really enjoy your writing and don't view it primarily as a professional responsibility, sit down and write.

Pick up your younger daughter from kindergarten—her sister, now in third grade, will be walking and talking with her friends—and hold her hand on the way home.

Relating

The time away from the classroom, between my illness and spring break, helped me begin to see an important shift I had been making over the course of the year—one that concerned my relationship with my students.

Before coming to Assumption, I saw myself as an explorer leading a band of shipmates on exciting intellectual journeys. I had studied the maps; I knew how to navigate; I had done the research, and my excitement and intellectual curiosity would inspire my crew to follow me into dark and mysterious places. They had signed up for the voyage, and I expected them to follow me willingly, even enthusiastically. After all, once we reached the new land, they would all have an equal share in the intellectual treasure.

But that relationship model didn't work for me and my students at Assumption—and won't work, I expect, for faculty at most colleges in the United States. Not all of these students, first of all, had willingly signed on for the journey. Some were on board because their parents had pushed them there; some were along for the shipboard parties; others saw their college courses as getting them from point A to point B and planned to jump ship at the first port—the promise of a secure job with a good salary. Of course there were exceptions, but many of them hadn't come on board for the sole purpose of accompanying me on journeys of intellectual discovery.

So I had to abandon that model, and the best replacement I could come up with to describe my role in the relationship that was evolving between me and my students was one that at first, I confess, stuck in my craw: I was like the coach of a high school sports team. We were a solid team with all the fundamental skills under our belt. Nothing too flashy—we weren't the state champions, but we weren't the conference doormats, either. My players came out for various reasons. Some were here out of inertia, because they had been playing the sport for a long time; others had been shoved onto the team by their parents; a few truly loved the sport; and one or two were capable of play at the professional level someday.

But this mix of players, with their different motivations and skill levels, meant that I had to focus my energies on four tasks: encouraging everyone into a love of the game, even if that meant jumping around and waving my arms during my halftime speech, or taking everyone out for pizza once in a while; drilling them on the basics, with daily practice; preparing them for the big games and evaluating their performance afterwards; and, finally, making sure they understood how playing the sport would benefit them throughout their lives.

So in March, following spring break, I begin to step more enthusiastically into the role of coach. I am coming to understand that if I want my students to participate in the discussions and exercises I plan, part of my job is to convince them that what we are doing *matters*—both in their future courses at the college and in their lives beyond college. My classroom practice slowly evolves from encouraging them to discuss interesting things to structuring discussions in which we practice the basic skills of my discipline: looking closely at texts, generating interpretations, and testing those interpretations against the words on the page and against each other. I make frequent mention of the relationship between specific classroom activities and what I will expect from them on their tests and papers, as well as—whenever possible—what employment or citizenship will demand from them beyond college. I start to wonder whether I should have been doing these same things with my students at Northwestern.

My three different class preparations (for four courses total) are spread across the major course divisions at the college—a freshman introductory course, an intermediate required course for majors, and an upper-level elective—making my efforts especially challenging. What works for one group of students doesn't always work for the others. So, just like last semester, I am still constantly working on course preparations, trying to find new ways to keep the students interested and to gear the classroom activities towards the development of specific analytic and interpretive skills.

On my second class day back in Introduction to Literature, for example, in mid-March, I begin our discussion of Ursula K. LeGuin's story "The Ones Who Walk Away from Omelas"—a philosophical fable in which a town's happiness depends entirely on keeping a small girl locked in a basement, in squalid conditions—with an activity I had once read about called the "concrete image" exercise. After introducing the story, I ask the students to clear their minds and think about the one most prominent concrete image of the story. Once they think of it, I tell them, write it down in as much detail as possible, then try to figure out how it helps you understand the meaning of the story.

(This counts as their weekly writing exercise, the substitute I have come up with for the quizzes that the president insisted were such a necessity. Once a week I pose a thought question at the beginning of class, one that requires them to write a full paragraph about a specific element of the story, in enough detail to demonstrate that they have read the material. It also requires them, though, to offer an in-depth analysis of that element, something that goes beyond mere description. I always use the question I pose for their weekly writing exercises as the first discussion question for that day.)

Once I have collected this exercise, I ask for volunteers to describe their images for me. Most of them focus on the girl, but they emphasize different elements of her condition, and I list these on the board. Once we have done that, I ask them to help me organize our images into a structure that will explain what the story means—and in the case of this philosophical fable, what lesson the author wants us to learn.

At the end of class, and it has been a good one, I make my pitch for the utility of what we have just done.

"This exercise," I explain, "models for you one way of analyzing a work of literature, and it's a way that you can and should be using in the papers you have due in a few weeks."

Ears prick up at this. I see some students pick up their pens and poise them over their notebooks.

"When you are reading a work of literature, keep your eye out for concrete images like these" (I gesture at the board), "for extremely detailed descriptions of objects or people or places, for the details that the author devotes a lot of attention to and that really stand out when you read. Those are the places to focus your attention when you are ready to start thinking about what the work means. Look closely at those details and images in the text, think about what they mean, analyze the specific word choices the author makes, and consider whether they represent more than what might first appear to you. Make a list of images or details that stand out, and do what we have just done here: try to find some principle that connects them, that organizes them.

"If you are reading something for the first time and you feel lost, look to the images and the details. And in your papers, always make sure that you are doing the sort of close analysis of those images and details that we have done here today."

More and more, as the semester proceeds, my classes begin to look like this. We spend time in class honing particular skills—skills that might seem specific to the art of literary interpretation, I tell them, but that will be required of them throughout their lives: reading closely, analyzing texts and situations, interpreting the written word, organizing their thoughts and words into papers and presentations.

I am doing the same thing, at another level, in the postcolonial-literature course, the upper-level elective in which I can count more on the students' understanding of what we are up to. In that class the students' most regular assignment is to write response papers, two-page analyses of a specific element of a novel. These analyses require them to focus on a short passage and analyze it in light of a broader theme in the novel. I designed the responses to help them learn one of the essential skills of writing papers of literary interpretation: close readings of specific passages from the text. But some of the students are still having trouble mastering the form, and I want to help them become better at it.

In mid-March we are reading E. M. Forster's *A Passage to India,* and they have a response paper due on the last class day we will spend on the novel. So for the second of the four classes we will devote to it, I have identified four passages that contain descriptions of the landscape or of significant characters in the novel.

"We are going to produce response papers here today," I tell them at the beginning of class, "and at the end of class we will talk together about how well we did."

I put the students into four pairs, assign each pair a passage, and ask them to highlight all the key words and phrases, explain what work these words and phrases are doing in the passage, and generate an interpretation of that passage in light of the themes in the novel we have discussed thus far. The results, when they report on their passage to the class, are mixed, but that doesn't matter. Together we all work to improve each interpretation and to link them to one another. Afterwards I emphasize that they can use the model of today's class when writing the individual response papers that will be due the following week.

Even in Argument and Persuasion, the writing course, I am moving more towards classroom activities that are warmups or even working sessions for the papers I have assigned. During a week in March when the students are preparing to write a paper about a campus policy issue, I begin class by showing some overheads I have developed that describe six different strategies for writing introductions and another six for writing conclusions. They take notes dutifully, writing down both the principles and the examples.

"OK," I say then, "open up to a fresh notebook page, choose one of the strategies I just described, and write an introduction to your paper." They are momentarily puzzled—you mean right here in class?— but then set to it, perhaps realizing that this will mean one less paragraph to write at 3 a.m. the day the paper is due. Fifteen minutes later they are mostly done, awaiting my next instructions.

"Good," I say. "Now choose a different strategy and write another introduction, completely different from your first one."

Another initial moment of puzzlement, then they set to again. Afterwards I have them show their two introductions to a couple of their peers and get feedback on which one caught people's attention and made them want to read on. In the final minutes of class I have a few people read their two introductions out loud, and we talk about them. At the end of the class I feel exhilarated. The lesson has gone exactly as I planned, I managed the clock so that we finished right on time, and I believe not only that have I taught my students something worth knowing, but also that they will actually remember it and apply it in their papers.

If I am proved right in this belief, it will be in part because of my decision to devote a good twenty-five to thirty minutes of a seventy-five-minute class to letting the students write. Earlier in my career I might have seen this as work they should be doing outside of class. But had I not added this component to the classroom lesson today, I now understand that some of them would have closed their notebooks on the introductory strategies I showed them and forgotten about them completely by the time they sat down to write the paper. All of them, now, have tried two of the strategies—those two at the very least, if not the other four, will have made a permanent impression.

In all three classes I increasingly find myself, at both the beginning and the end of class, explaining the reasons for what we are doing. I am sure some of them see these explanations as just another few minutes of talk that they don't have to take notes on, but many of our students, and most of our majors, are preparing for careers in education. When I make these explanations, I sometimes see those students nodding their heads, as if recognizing for the first time that what we are doing in class makes sense and may even prove useful someday in their careers.

I still have classes that fail abysmally, of course, and this usually happens when I take a technique that worked well in one class and try to plop it unmodified into a different class.

Remembering my success with Beethoven's "Ode to Joy" in Contemporary British Fiction, I try the same thing in Postcolonial Literature when we come to the literature of India. I play a piece by Ravi Shankar and give the same instructions: listen to it and write down the adjectives that come to your mind that mirror adjectives we have heard our writers using about India.

Everyone writes down the same two or three words, and it takes all of two minutes to get those out and on the board. Perhaps the class is too small for this kind of exercise, or perhaps I didn't think it through enough for this new context. I also don't understand Indian music very well, and I may have ventured too far out of my field. But I don't worry too much about it. I chalk it up as a failed experiment, and hey—it filled up fifteen minutes of class time.

But failures like this come less frequently as my understanding of my relationship with my students continues to develop. So despite the time commitments—still overwhelming and substantially increased from last semester—a very small corner of my brain recognizes that I am getting better at this.

Seven months into my first year of full-time teaching, I am also beginning to see how students' relationships with each other have an impact on what we do in the classroom.

Assumption has very little demographic diversity. I have not yet had an African-American student in my class. I had one student with a vaguely Hispanic name, but he was light-skinned, and nothing in his speech or dress hinted at his ethnic identity. What really shocks me is that I have had no Asian students. At Northwestern, Asians and Asian-Americans made up a substantial portion of the student body, and I assumed that this was a national trend. I see now that I was very mistaken.

So I have no complications in classroom relations that arise from dealing with an ethnically diverse student body. What I have instead are the complications of dealing with students of both genders—complications that appear to me as complications only in this second semester, when I have one class with only female students (Postcolonial Literature), one with a majority of female students (Argument and Persuasion), and two that are equally divided or slightly tipped towards male students.

Argument and Persuasion perhaps offers me the best lesson in how male students change the dynamics of a classroom discussion. I have scheduled three or four debates during the semester—classes in which the students have done some reading on a controversial issue the night before, then come in prepared to state and defend their opinions. I ask them to write down an explanation for their position at the beginning of class—I collect these position statements and count them as their writing exercise grade—and then we divide up the room and people choose to sit on one side or the other, depending upon the position they support.

Even though only a handful of students in the class are male, they dominate those debate sessions. They state their positions forcefully, sometimes even mocking the positions of the other side or asking pointed questions in response to a comment from someone on the other side. The women never do this. They offer guarded, neutral statements of their position and never confront each other or the men directly. A good half-dozen of the women try to avoid entering the debate at all, and I have to coax them in occasionally by asking, as genially as possible, why they chose to sit on that particular side.

These behaviors conform to stereotypes we have about men and women, but they also conform to descriptions I have read about the difference in learning preferences between men and women. Part of me doesn't want to accept those stereotypes or descriptions, but I can't ignore what I see in the classroom. I am glad that I have scheduled only a few debates for the semester, because I begin to sense that the men are—unintentionally, I think—intimidating the women enough to keep them from speaking in class more generally.

I don't want this to happen, because in the class sessions in which we are not debating, and in my other three classes as well, the women contribute to the discussion more frequently, and more thoughtfully, than the men—and this was true in my fall-semester classes as well. They are far more likely to raise their hands and speculate about an answer, or to offer answers that suggest to me that they are working towards an idea rather than stating a fully formed opinion. I like that and want to encourage it as much as possible, since I see one goal of our discussions as being to move us all towards ideas and perspectives we haven't yet thought of.

I can see the problem in its most dramatic form in the two students who are taking both Argument and Persuasion and the all-female Postcolonial Literature. Both of them participate regularly in Postcolonial Literature but do so very rarely, or only when called upon, in Argument and Persuasion. Part of that reluctance may be due to class size; they may be less willing to speak in front of a larger group. But I suspect that's not the only reason. It feels to me sometimes as if the men have marked Argument and Persuasion as their territory, and those two female students feel constrained.

Of course exceptions exist to these generalizations. I have one female student in Argument and Persuasion who holds her ground with the men and argues as forcefully and aggressively as they do. I will see her in several more of my classes in the coming years, and she is destined—no surprise—for law school. One or two more of her type might have changed the dynamic of that class, but she stands alone.

My faculty colleagues talk about the culture of silence we have here on campus and complain about students' unwillingness to participate in class. I have been fighting that silence all semester and am convinced that the fault lies more with the faculty than the students; we are not trying hard enough to draw them into the conversation. But the small share of the blame that does fall onto the students, I have come to feel by the middle of the spring semester, somehow relates to this gender dynamic.

This awareness will establish in me a preference for classes in which the students are predominantly female. In the future, when I get my class lists the week before the semester starts, the first thing I will do is run down the list, counting the numbers of women and men in each course. If at least two-thirds of the names aren't female, I begin thinking immediately about how I will have to work a little harder in that course to create the open and participatory culture I try to cultivate in my classrooms.

If I could think of a way to promote more of the sort of dialogue I like to hear in the classroom, without letting the voices of the male students dominate, I would try it. But I can't see how to do that yet and resolve to keep thinking about it.

Finally, in a third form of relating, I am now starting to identify certain well-defined types of students, and to develop individual relationships with these students and others that are novel and sometimes puzzling to me.

Some of the most puzzling elements emerge as a result of my attendance policy. While I tend to run a very laid-back classroom, I am a stickler about attendance. I teach by means of discussion and interactive exercises, and people have to be in the seats in order for those activities to work. So I state on my syllabus that students get two or three free passes for their first absences (depending upon whether the class meets two or three times per week), but that I will lower their attendance and participation grade (which accounts for 10 percent of their final grade) by one letter for each subsequent absence.

I am a little conflicted about this policy, because as an undergraduate I would have viewed it as both petty and draconian. And in fact I skipped classes regularly. I took a philosophy course once in which the professor had given a big speech about attendance at the beginning of the semester. I ignored the speech and one spring day spent the hour of that class taking a nap on my couch. At the end of the hour I was awakened by a phone call from him, asking where I had been. For the rest of the semester I viewed him as a petty schoolmaster.

So attendance policies have become yet another area, like my work with the English Club, in which I have to reconcile myself to playing roles I would have scorned as an undergraduate.

Tamara, a student in the upper-level class, becomes the first person to trigger the grade penalization that my attendance policy outlines. I was happy to meet her at the beginning of the semester and welcomed her presence in class, because Tamara doesn't look like every other student on campus. Assumption students tend to dress and present themselves in similar ways, either preppy or jeans-and-t-shirt casual. Tamara comes to class smelling of cigarettes and wearing Birkenstocks, baggy t-shirts, and pajama bottoms (the classroom is actually in a student dormitory, and she lives just down the hall). In her papers and in class discussions she often makes observations that surprise both me and her fellow students. She is what we would have called, when I was an undergraduate, a granola.

As an undergraduate, I admired the granolas. I idealized them as the rebels of our generation, the ones who had the courage to reject mainstream values and to show it in their appearance. I shared their mentality but was too lazy to cultivate any particular look. I wore the clothes I got for Christmas every year (mostly jeans and t-shirts). As a student, I would probably have been a little in love with Tamara and her unconventionality.

As a professor, though, I find her frustrating. She misses class more frequently than any student I have had thus far at Assumption. She has turned in two assignments late, once without clearing it with me in advance (something I require for late papers). Her writing exercises and her occasional silent days tell me that she does the reading only half the time.

The very same commitment to unconventionality and to rejecting mainstream values that I so admire in her motivates her to reject my policies as well. I understand this, but it still frustrates me. Please, I want to tell her, be as unconventional as possible outside my classroom—but in here you have to do as I say. By the middle of the semester I am wishing that Tamara, whose attitude and look I had seen as a welcome break from the conformity of her fellow students, would flaunt her rebellion in someone else's classroom.

I am having a similar problem with a student in Argument and Persuasion. Beth is an extremely talented writer who has been receiving some of the highest grades in class. She is very friendly and usually has intelligent comments to make in class. I like her both as a person and as a student and have spoken to her about signing up for the creative nonfiction class I will be teaching in the fall. I see her name around campus occasionally, in the newspaper or in e-mails from the Student Government Association, so I know she maintains a strong presence in campus activities.

She doesn't have quite as strong a presence in my classroom, though, and by midsemester she has missed a week and a half's worth of class. I suspect that Tamara skips class for no good reason and is probably sitting in her room with her friends and her bong while my students are puzzling over Ravi Shankar (although it wouldn't surprise me to discover that Tamara was also listening to Ravi Shankar at the same time, if in a slightly altered state of consciousness). But given Beth's talent and evident interest in the course, I assume that she is missing class for a good reason. Maybe she has overcommitted herself to student government activities, for example.

I am disabused of this notion one spring day when I receive an e-mail from her in the morning saying that she is feeling ill and doesn't want to risk getting out of bed.

"Thanks for letting me know," I write back. "I hope you feel better."

I go and teach class, and on my way back from class I take a route across the center of campus that I don't usually take. I am walking along, thinking about my lunch, when I see Beth, with just-showered wet hair and an armful of books, two hundred yards away and coming towards me on a parallel path. I'm so surprised that I can't help but stare. At around a hundred yards away she catches a glimpse of me out of the corner of her eye. She freezes, then runs off perpendicular to the path, into the library.

I find this both amusing and depressing: amusing that she thought it necessary to run away from me, but depressing in that I now have concrete evidence that she lied to me. Of course I told lies as an undergraduate too—I told that philosophy professor who phoned me that I had been working to finish a paper for another class and lost track of time—so I can't say that I lose all respect for Beth. But it's one thing to know theoretically that students lie to professors; it's quite another to find evidence that someone has lied to you.

Both Tamara and Beth, when they come to class, are competent students. So although they are presenting challenging new relationships to me, they are not challenging my pedagogical skills.

That has been left to Mary, the student who has followed me from Freshman Composition to Introduction to Literature. Mary's writing has proved impervious to my semester and a half's worth of commentary and instruction. No matter what I tell her in my comments or in class, she continues to turn in the same labored prose.

Because of the weeks I missed for class, which included some time I should have spent helping them prepare to write their papers, I have given the students in Introduction to Literature the option to rewrite their second papers for a better grade, as long as they come see me in my office to talk about their revision plans.

Mary, who received a low C on her paper, makes an appointment. In my office I work slowly through the paper with her, explaining to her the larger areas—structure, focus, use of evidence—on which she should concentrate her attention. She nods, looking at her paper, and hardly says a word.

The sad truth—and I find this very disconcerting—is that Mary needs more help than I have the time and energy to give her. She doesn't understand sentence structure; her papers are littered with sentence fragments and comma splices. She doesn't understand how to use evidence; the passages she quotes have no relation to her point. She doesn't understand how to use transitional words or sentences; she just piles one short sentence on top of another, and if two sentences or paragraphs ever appear to be related, it's probably coincidental.

Since my time at the Searle Center, I have had a fairly idealistic view of teaching. If a student is not being reached, I always assume, it's because the teacher is not doing his job or has not yet found the right method. But I've tried everything I can think of with Mary, and nothing works. It's not stupidity; the problem lies with her attitude. Her apathy seems carefully cultivated. She seems afraid of seeming too interested in school, for reasons I can't fathom.

After my meeting with her, I sit back in my recliner and finally allow to emerge in my conscious brain a sentiment that has been lurking below the surface for a while: I give up on Mary. Something between us doesn't fit. She and I are never going to have our triumphant breakthrough. Maybe if she were my only student, I could reach her someday and persuade her to care enough to make the effort she would need to succeed in my class. But not this year, and not this semester. Maybe Mary is a genius at math or science, disciplines in which I might appear as hopeless to her as she does to me. But I won't ever find that out. I hope I never see her in class again.

The one student from Introduction to Literature whom I do hope to see in class again, Krystan, announces to me in my office one afternoon in March that she is transferring. Assumption offers only one course in the subject she wants to study, and no major.

I'm really sorry to hear this, because Krystan is brilliant. She wrote the only A paper I have seen in class so far this semester (I have given out a few A-minuses, but only this one A). She always does the reading, she aces all the quizzes, she writes beautiful papers, and she regularly offers thoughtful contributions in class. I've been disappointed on the one or two days she has missed class, knowing that the quality of the discussion will probably descend a peg or two. She speaks in a high, breathy voice, sits in the front row, and takes assiduous notes. She comes to see me at least twice before each paper is due—a completely unnecessary ritual, since the first drafts she shows me are always A papers already.

As soon as she tells me the school to which she is transferring, and the reason for her choice, I realize that she is making the right decision. I would never say that Krystan, or any student, is too good for Assumption, because I believe that I and my colleagues have much to offer to even the most brilliant of students. But Krystan could be earning A's at Harvard or Yale, she has a well thought out desire to study a subject offered only at schools like Harvard and Yale, and she really should go.

Still, I hate to see her leave. During her office visits I have been talking to her about majoring in English, and I had hopes of seeing her in my classes for the next three years. I mention the possibility that the college would probably allow her to cobble together a major with courses taken from the local consortium we belong to, but she has clearly made up her mind.

She is a hard student to let go, because she makes my job so much more interesting and enjoyable. Although I don't have much time or energy to devote to recruiting talented students into the college and the major, the luxury of having a student like Krystan in my classroom helps me understand the importance of doing just that. In the future, when students like her come to my office, I will take more time with them than usual, asking them about their interests and trying to forge relationships that will leave them with positive feelings about the school and the major.

My favorite student this semester, though, is Dana, a sophomore who for some reason is taking Introduction to Literature (a course required for freshmen). Dana is stocky and large, with a crewcut and glasses. He never carries more than a book and notebook into class, an anomaly amid the rows of overflowing backpacks. He shuffles from side to side as he walks and greets everyone—me, his fellow students—with a wide grin and "How ya' doin'?"

He is likable, first of all. He pays attention in class, volunteers in discussion, and is the only one who laughs at my most obscure jokes. But the best thing about Dana is that he is *interesting*. He reads literature outside of class. He writes poetry. His comments in class occasionally reveal a deep interest in, and familiarity with, theology and philosophy. He reminds me of myself as an undergraduate in some respects, although he is far more jovial and extroverted than I was or ever will be. As with Tamara, I can tell that sometimes Dana hasn't done the reading, and he has missed a few classes. But he turns in his work on time, raises the level and quality of discussion, and writes decent papers, so I am willing to grant him a little leeway.

I would love to sit down with Dana at a bar sometime—and from the conversations I overhear before and after class, it is evident that he spends time in bars—so that I could talk to him outside the normal framework of student–teacher interactions. I bet he tells great stories, and I am curious about his parents and his background, and about what led him to Assumption College. But I know enough not to invite students to bars, and to be honest I am not very socially adept or good at making small talk. So I doubt Dana and I will end up as pals.

Still, he is one of a number of students in whom I see a spark of something that really catches my attention, and I wish I could find ways to get to know them on a more personal level. At this point in my career, though, I am not yet sure enough of the appropriate boundaries between students and faculty to risk crossing them in an effort to get to know my students outside of the classroom. I hope that this knowledge will come to me with time, and perhaps with tenure.

As an undergraduate myself, I wasn't interested in interacting with my professors outside the classroom. I was curious about their lives but would have felt uncomfortable in social situations with them. Perhaps my reluctance or inability to connect with my students more fully outside the classroom stems from my memory of that attitude in myself, and from an assumption that my students feel the same way I did back then.

And indeed, in this second semester I am coming to understand how much my undergraduate attitudes about students and teachers and education have colored—and in many cases warped—my current perspectives.

I don't know whether I am alone in this, but a part of me has always felt that the undergraduate Jim Lang sets a good standard for the values and behavior of the older Jim Langs who have come along since then. I was an idealist in college, and I remain one; I hate it when people snidely dismiss the idealism of their youth. I still believe in the power of ideas to change the world. That belief is part of what keeps me in this business.

But by the middle of my second semester I am becoming more and more aware that the undergraduate Jim Lang, whose idealism I still admire, did not have the knowledge or experience to be a good judge of pedagogical practices or student relations. He didn't understand classroom dynamics; he would never have seen how his own assertive voice might intimidate others; he would have dismissed as silly or timid anyone who feared joining a classroom conversation. He was the product of an all-male high school and a male-oriented culture of sports and Catholicism at Notre Dame. He would have groaned and rolled his eyes at the sorts of exercises I regularly conduct to make students comfortable and open to discussion in my classrooms.

He wasn't exactly an idiot, but he had his blinders.

Understanding my relationships with my students more clearly, and learning to manage them more effectively, has meant sloughing off some pieces of that old Jim Lang and coming to realize that his experiences out there in the seats don't always serve me very well up here in front of the blackboard.

I have watched colleagues go through similar realizations and have watched others who never come to see that their experiences in college or graduate school should not necessarily form the measuring stick for their own teaching practices. Many of us who entered Ph.D. programs did so because we learned best by means of reading and listening to lecturers. But many students out in the seats in liberal arts colleges like mine don't learn best by those means, and they need more interactive and hands-on forms of teaching.

The most complex relationship I find myself having to negotiate in my continued development as a teacher, then, is the one between my past and present selves.

Figuring It Out,
Parts One & Two

Figuring It Out, Part One. In late March the chair of the department informs the junior members of the faculty that a proposal has been put forward by one of our senior colleagues to form a new committee within the department. The committee's role will be to provide mentoring for junior faculty and to help them understand what they should be doing to prepare for their upcoming tenure bids.

Theoretically, this seems like a sensible recommendation. After all, I have been teaching for almost seven months now and have received no official feedback on how I am doing. Nobody has spoken with me about what I should be doing during this first year to ensure my tenure, and of course this college—like every college—has no specific set of guidelines for me to follow.

But despite the good sense of our senior colleague's suggestion, all of us—Mark, Ed, Charles, and I—decide that we would rather not see such a committee formed. Dan, the other junior faculty member, doesn't really enter into this discussion, probably because he is making his tenure bid this year and his fortunes are already determined.

Mark and I have the same two objections to the proposal, one theoretical and one practical:

1. Theoretical: Why do we need a committee to formalize mentoring relationships that could be more appropriately conducted on an informal, one-on-one basis with senior faculty members we already feel comfortable going to for advice?

2. Practical: More *(heavy sigh)* meetings.

The practical point probably weighs more heavily on my mind than the theoretical one. Even though such meetings could ultimately help me secure my future at Assumption, I am so tapped out at this point in the academic year that the thought of one more meeting makes me want to burst into tears. I am still recuperating from my week in the hospital, so physical fatigue may be playing a role, but I have felt overwhelmed by meetings and service obligations all year and can't stomach the thought of any more.

I'm not sure why Charles dislikes the proposal, since he keeps his cards pretty close to his vest. Ed seems especially concerned about it, for reasons that aren't clear to me.

The chair has invited us to lunch to talk about it, because she wants us to be prepared when it comes up at the next departmental meeting. I gather from this advance warning that she doesn't think much of the proposal either, although again I don't know why.

"Why are they doing this now?" Ed asks her at the lunch meeting. "Are we in trouble? Do they think one of us is likely to have our tenure bid rejected?"

The chair reassures him that this is not the case. But in the following days Ed seems preoccupied with the matter. He tells both Mark and me, in separate conversations, that he sees something sinister in it, even if he can't put his finger on just what it might be. As best I can tell, he believes that the senior faculty are using this proposal as an attempt to exercise control over us and the department.

While I can see this interpretation as a theoretical possibility, one fact prevents me from buying it: the proposal was presented by Maurice, the one member of the department who is respected by everybody, who gets along with everybody, and who does not have a sinister cell in his body. However much I may disagree with the proposal, its origin with Maurice convinces me that it is at least well intentioned.

For that reason, I don't buy into Ed's suspicions. However, my conversation with him helps me understand another reason I don't support the proposal, one I could never articulate to my senior colleagues—and one I am pretty sure my junior colleagues share.

My senior colleagues and I have different views of what Assumption

College, and the English department, should look like. I want the school to place more emphasis on research and publication, to reward research and publication with grants and course releases. They, from what I have been able to tell, want the institution to maintain its current emphasis on teaching over research. I understand this. Having earned tenure at an institution that rewarded them for successful teaching, they don't want suddenly to be told to intensify their efforts in what has so far been a secondary concern in their academic careers. But even though I understand their perspective, I don't share it, so I am probably resisting this proposal because I don't want some committee pressuring me to de-emphasize a part of my academic life that matters to me as much as my teaching does.

The difference between my perspective on the proposed committee and Ed's is that I don't see my senior colleagues' motives as sinister and controlling. It is hard to imagine the amicable colleagues I work with every day as sinister, and they are controlling only in the sense that we all try to control our environments—Ed or I as much as anyone. Ed sometimes hints darkly that he knows things I don't, and that if I had the same knowledge I would feel the same way. But I don't have that knowledge and don't want to make judgments based on second- or thirdhand reports of old conflicts.

The department meets in late March, on a Wednesday afternoon at four. I taught two classes that morning and met my independent-study student at one o'clock. My time in the hospital is only a month behind me, so I'm still pretty worn out by the end of the day. I have the best intentions to attend a lecture tonight by a visiting rabbi but already doubt that I will feel up to returning to campus at seven.

The meeting begins with the usual laundry list of announcements and calls for volunteers for various committees. We agree on a mass and a donation for a deceased former member of the department; we need people to staff the English table at the college's Open House and to serve on the planning committee for a dinner we hold for our senior majors in late spring; we review our library allocations and learn how much money we have left to spend on ordering library books for the year. Then a couple of academic matters: settling what requirement a particular course should fulfill, then discussing a concern the dean has about the number of independent studies being offered by the department.

Finally, under New Business, at around 5 p.m.—just fifteen minutes before the scheduled close of the meeting—the chair cedes the floor to Maurice, who makes his recommendation that the department form a subcommittee of tenured members to come up with guidelines to help untenured faculty in their progress towards tenure.

The idea for such a committee, he explains, came to him during the interview phase of the provost search the college is currently conducting. Maurice is a member of the search committee. One of the candidates asked the committee what sort of mentoring the departments provided to help junior faculty prepare for tenure. Hearing that we had no formal system, the candidate said that he would definitely work to institute one if he was hired.

That provost search proved unsuccessful, and the installation of a new provost will have to wait another year. But Maurice doesn't see why we shouldn't form a mentoring program in the English department this year.

The chair opens the meeting for discussion of the proposal. I am prepared to disagree as nicely as possible, citing the one objection I can express publicly: that while I appreciate the sentiment behind the proposal, such a committee doesn't seem necessary, since I feel comfortable approaching individual senior colleagues for help. (I have no intention, of course, of delving into the clash-of-academic-values argument.) But as a first-year faculty member, I don't want to react too negatively to a proposal made by a senior colleague I respect. So I'm hoping someone else will speak up against the proposal and I won't have to.

Mark offers the first demurral.

"I'm grateful for this idea," he says, "and I would have no objection to a committee like this. I could definitely use any help people are willing to offer." Smiles at Mark's light self-deprecation. "But I also want to say that I don't feel that this is necessary to me, at least at this stage of my career. I would be comfortable asking advice from people on things I was confused or concerned about, and I would hate to put another layer of committees between us and the senior faculty, if we can just do it on a more informal basis."

I steel myself. If Mark can do it, so can I.

"I agree," I say. "I appreciate the fact that you want to help us, and I wouldn't have any objections if the committee were formed. But I feel comfortable enough with my senior colleagues that I would go to them for help and advice if I needed it. We could certainly do this in the form of a committee, but I personally don't feel that I need a committee to get mentoring from you. And it may be just the end of the first year talking," I add with a smile, "but at this moment the idea of another set of committee meetings to attend seems . . . daunting."

People smile and nod understandingly.

"Can I ask something?" Ed asks when I am finished. He speaks directly to Maurice. "Is there some reason why this has come up now? Do you have concerns about us? Is there some reason why you think we need this mentoring right now? Has something come up, or someone said something about any of us?"

"No, of course not," Maurice responds. He explains again about the provost search committee and adds that he really felt that the department could do more to help us get through the difficult tenure process. Laura seconds his point, and it becomes clear from the detailed nature of her response that she too has played a part in formulating the proposal.

At that point Charles steps in. He will tell me later that he thought Mark and I had responded too gently. He too would have preferred to offer a gentle response, but he had no intention of walking out of that room until the proposal had been shot down.

Charles begins by echoing the points Mark and I made, then he steps up the rhetoric.

"I believe completely that you are making this proposal with the best of intentions," he says, leaning back in his chair and looking around the room, over everyone's heads. "But a proposal like this looks very different to us than it does to you. From our perspective, no matter what you intend by it, this proposal looks like an effort to exercise control over us. You will be telling us what we should be doing. We will have to listen. We will have no choice, since you will be voting on our tenure in a few years.

"We are not in equal positions of power. That's fine. But if you come and tell us that you want this committee formed, and that you plan to tell us what we should be doing to get tenure, you are exercising your power over us. It will never *feel* to us the way it was *intended* by you."

I can see now that Charles feels exactly as I do about the clash of values between the senior and junior members of the department. I am impressed, and a little shocked, that he has addressed the issue so openly. It makes me wonder, again, whether Charles is long for this college. Would he speak so openly to his senior colleagues if he intended to stay here?

Laura responds in a voice literally choking with emotion.

"I can't believe," she says, "I just can't *believe*, that you would have these kinds of fears and suspicions about a proposal that was raised by Maurice. We have none of these intentions you are talking about. This is not about us exercising control over you, or power. This is about *helping* you. We don't want to *tell* you what to do. We want to hear what your concerns and questions are, and be able to address them. We want to *listen* to you."

And then, for reasons I still don't understand, something ruptures the emotional dams of one of our colleagues, and we all watch as two years' worth of grievances, suspicions, hurt feelings, and suppressed tensions spill out onto the table before us and sweep away what's left of the meeting. Literally shouting, he hurls personal insults and professional accusations at colleagues seated across the table. The chair tries to intervene, threatening to stop the meeting, but she cannot stem the tide of his emotions, and his shouting drowns her out.

The tirade, occasionally interrupted by the brief denials of the multiple (and multiply) accused, goes on for a good thirty minutes—the worst thirty minutes of my life, to this very day. I keep my eyes glued to the table. I can't believe this is happening, and I keep praying, futilely, for it to end.

The meeting ends at 6 p.m., with voices now quieter but fresh blood on the table, spilled from wounds that will never fully heal. The proposal that sparked the melee is already a distant memory. It will never be mentioned again.

Mark and I walk out together, in total shock, and linger at our cars wondering what just happened. We are thinking the same thing: How stupid are we, not to have seen these tensions before? And even scarier: Did we make a huge mistake by accepting jobs in this department?

It takes Mark and me weeks to sort through our intellectual and emotional appraisals of the meeting, and we talk about it in our offices and on walks together to the cafeteria or to class. We eventually figure two things out.

The first is that we have both spent eight months imagining that we had lucked into a collegial paradise. We understand now that this fantasy stemmed partially from naivete. We have both worked office jobs and should have realized that antagonisms and grievances color the relationships in every work situation.

The fantasy stemmed too from the fact that we have simply not had the time or mental energy to pay enough attention to departmental relations to see them clearly. Mark and I have spent a lot of time talking to each other in and outside of our offices, since we have had so many shared experiences of our first year both to rejoice and to commiserate about. We have spent far less time in the offices of our peers.

And our colleagues, it now becomes apparent to us, have been doing their best to keep their squabbles out of our view. This is understandable. Other people's disagreements always seem petty to an outsider, and no one wants the grievances that create these little squabbles laid out for public viewing. I don't know whether they imagined they could conceal their divisions from us forever, but no matter. The veils have been torn away.

Our second realization concerns the territory behind those veils, which we now see has distinct divides. In my first semester, if I ever sensed tension between individuals in the department, I simply attributed it to the tension that might arise between two people arguing over something they both care about. In the arguments for the candidates in February, in which rancor and old grievances remained still half-hidden behind neutral rhetoric, we saw that there were at least two different schools of thought about the future of the department and the college. But now that we have seen a battle fought on open ground, it isn't hard to cast our minds back to the various proposals we have debated over the course of the year and to see how certain people have tended—as if they were students preparing for a debate in Argument and Persuasion—to sit on one side of the room of any issue, and certain people on the other.

The meeting didn't do much to enlighten us about the causes of the divide that separates the two major camps, and it will be another year or two before we learn the shadow history of the department that forged these divisions and alliances. They certainly go far deeper than I had imagined in February, when I saw them as stemming from different perspectives on the college's emphasis on teaching over research. But Mark and I are now able to run down the list of people in the department and in most cases identify the alliance to which they belong. Not everyone falls into a camp: Maurice seems above it all, and Charles does his best to fly under the radar, so I can't place him in one camp or the other.

And in fact I figure one more thing out, at the end of April, about Charles and his way of conducting himself in the department.

During my first eight months at Assumption, I have regarded Charles as someone who looks out only for himself, who deliberately keeps a low profile in order to avoid having to express opinions that might offend someone—an attitude that strikes me as cowardly and selfish. My opinion of him isn't helped by the fact that he and I are both quiet, reserved types and so haven't been inclined to spill our darkest secrets to each other over coffee. He also has a baby at home and never makes it out with the rest of us when we meet at the bar.

I was surprised and grateful when he spoke up at the meeting and am confident that we could have killed that proposal on the strength of his rhetoric, had the subsequent outburst not effectively washed it away. And as the semester comes to a close and I look back at what I have seen of Charles, I realize that I have misjudged him. I realize, indeed, that he is the one member of the department whose behavior I should emulate.

One of Mark's friends, a senior economist at a state university in California, gave him some advice when Mark accepted the job at Assumption, and Mark later shared it with me. All first-year assistant professors come into their new schools, he said, and try to remake their departments in the image of their graduate-school departments. Of course that never works. The right behavior, according to the economist, is to keep your mouth shut for your entire first year. Listen to what is going on around you, think about it, but don't show any of your own cards until the start of your second year.

Our chair has made it difficult for us to follow these instructions to the letter, since she began soliciting our opinions about departmental matters at those first day-long meetings back in August. But I realize that I have spent too much time trying to formulate my positions on departmental issues in this first year, a time when I have little or no influence with my colleagues in and out of the department. That time would have been better spent as I now see Charles has been spending it: listening, analyzing, and thinking—not about what we were voting on, but about how votes were being conducted, and who was voting for what and why. Had I been doing so more assiduously, I might not have been so stunned when the departmental landscape suddenly fissured at my feet.

We have one more meeting scheduled for the end of the year, and I vow to spend that meeting as I should have been spending the first half-dozen of them, and as all first-year faculty members should spend their opening year of departmental meetings: with my head down, my mouth shut, and my eyes and ears wide open.

Figuring It Out, Part Two. The revelation of these difficult departmental relations, along with my illness and fragile physical state, could have led to a pretty awful climax to my first year on the tenure track. But that doesn't happen, thanks to the drama, quite literally, of the final weeks of April.

My month of drama actually begins in early April, when Anne and I attend the student production of *One Flew over the Cuckoo's Nest* with Mark. The students do an incredible job with the story, playing the roles with energy and talent. One young man with a shaved head, playing one of the mental patients, darts hilariously in and out of the audience during the hectic party scene at the play's climax, and the student playing Nurse Ratched acts her role with arch precision, as the part demands.

As the play unfolds before me, I am struck again with the sentiment that followed the lecture I attended in the fall: I have joined a thriving cultural and intellectual community, one that has a tremendous amount to offer me when I can find the time to take advantage of it. I recommit myself to taking advantage of it as often as possible.

Around the time I see the play, we have finished poetry and fiction in Introduction to Literature and have moved on to the third genre of the semester, drama. We are spending one day on a short play by a contemporary female playwright, then two weeks on Shakespeare's *Othello*. This imbalance in focus reflects the complexity of the assignment they will be completing this unit: identify a scene from *Othello* that is central to understanding one of the play's major themes, work with a group to translate that scene into modern American English, then stage that contemporary-language scene for the class. On the final day of the productions (for which I have reserved two classes), all students will also turn in a two-page paper analyzing how their scene contributes to our understanding of one of the main themes of the plays we have discussed.

We start by spending four days discussing *Othello*. This goes very slowly at first, in large part because of the language of the play, which they—like every other high school and college student in America—have some trouble understanding. So I spend the first day establishing the basics of the setting, the plot, and the characters and their relationships with one another. We have a lot of exchanges that go like this:

> *Professor:* OK, let's look at the first exchanges here between Iago and Roderigo. Can you tell me from this dialogue one reason why Iago hates Othello?
>
> *Student [tentatively]:* Because he wanted to be his lieutenant, and Othello gave the job to Cassio?
>
> *Professor:* Right. But can you point me to the specific line that tells you that?
>
> *Student [looking at his text]:* Ummmmm . . . "Three great ones of the city, / In personal suit to make me his lieutenant, / Off-capp'd to him . . ."
>
> *Professor:* Good. And what does "off-capp'd" mean?
>
> *[Silence.]*
>
> *Professor:* C'mon, now. Somebody just take a guess.
>
> *Different student [very tentatively]:* Kissed his butt?
>
> *Professor:* Right. OK, now can anyone tell me the second reason Iago hates Othello?

And so on. It's not the most exciting classroom work, but it's necessary groundwork for understanding the play, and I much prefer it to just lecturing them on the background. This way at least I know their brains are engaged.

In the last part of class, looking forward to their assignment, I pick a short speech by Othello and ask them to translate it into modern English.

I have a few of them read their speeches out loud, and I comment on the parts that I thought were well done.

The class goes fairly well—by which I mean that a good dozen different students participated in the conversation—but the students as a class did not seem to reach their usual energy level, and I assume they are still daunted by the language and not much interested in the play at this point. So for the second day I pull out the best friend of everyone who has to teach this generation of connoisseurs of the visual: I bring in a couple of videos.

I have two different movie versions of the play, an older one starring Anthony Hopkins as Othello and a newer version with Lawrence Fishburne in the role. I identify a two-scene sequence in which Iago, Othello's malevolent and slighted ensign, coaxes a rival into a drunken brawl, which brings down the wrath of Othello on the rival. Iago finishes the scene with a sinister monologue outlining his plot to achieve Othello's downfall. In these scenes Hopkins plays the title role with majesty and detachment, an aristocrat rather than a soldier; Fishburne is a warrior, his emotions raw and brutal. I show the class both scenes and ask them as they watch to write down the significant differences between the two versions, from the depictions of Othello and Iago to the details of the setting.

Afterwards we make a list of the major differences on the board—a long list, which indicates to me that they watched closely. I eye the list carefully when we are done, circle "Draws his sword" under the Fishburne version, and ask them to tell me how it affects their understanding of the play.

"It shows he's a soldier," says one student, "that he solves his problems by fighting first. The other guy seemed like more of a talker."

"And it shows he gets angry real easy," another student adds. "He can't control his emotions very well. The other Othello seemed like he never really got angry."

"Excellent," I say. "Now remember that when we come to the end, and see which of those two Othellos makes more sense in light of what Othello does at the conclusion of the play."

I repeat this same exercise for several more differences we have identified. I emphasize at the end of class how important these decisions about character and staging are to a dramatic production.

The two scenes we witnessed were so different that I am certain they have understood that point, and so now I am hopeful about their dramatic productions. On the third day we finish our discussion of the play, and on the fourth day I allow them to spend most of the class time working in their groups on their translations and the planning of their scenes. I have papers to grade for Argument and Persuasion that week, so having one day for which I do not have to prepare a lesson plan has turned out to be extremely helpful.

On Wednesday morning I come in not really knowing what to expect. One of the first groups to present is Krystan's, the brilliant woman who will be leaving Assumption this semester, and her group has selected the famous scene in which Iago first plants in Othello's mind the seeds of suspicion about his wife's fidelity. They have sensibly chosen to use the shyest of the three women in the group as the narrator. Reading from her script in a quiet monotone, she begins by introducing the scene and explaining its importance.

Then, to my amazement, I see the scene come to life. Krystan plays Othello, and she does it with incredible intensity and emotion. She uses a chair as her only prop and alternately sits and stands, stalking Iago around the room with her questions. When Othello explodes into rage, she stomps her foot on the floor and screams. (For a moment I cringe, wondering what the teacher next door will think, but then I get over it. Hey, we're learning in here.) The actors occasionally pause to allow the narrator to step in and explain the reasons for their translation or staging choices. I am really impressed by the quality of their analysis, their translation, and even the acting.

I am equally impressed by the antics of Dana's group, which chooses to act out the scene we had watched twice on video, which begins with a drinking game and ends in a brawl. They set the scene in a contemporary college dorm room. Their translations are loose, with original dialogue such as this:

Iago: Come, lieutenant, I have a stope of wine, and here without are a brace of Cyprus gallants that would fain have a measure to the health of black Othello.

Cassio: Not to-night, good Iago, I have very poor and unhappy brains for

ॐ

drinking. I could well wish courtesy would invent some other custom of entertainment.

ending up like this:

> *Iago:* C'mon, Cassio, everybody's playing beer pong. We're all getting loaded; come have a few coldies with us.
> *Cassio:* No way, dude. I'm still hanging from last night. I'm just gonna chill.

With ping-pong paddles, a ball, and a few empty cups, they simulate the college drinking game "beer pong" on my desk. But the production really gets going when the brawl starts and they pull out toy swords dug out of someone's attic and start prancing around the room, plastic blades clacking against one another in a passable version of a drunken sword fight.

The students in the audience keep giving me furtive looks, not sure whether the student actors have crossed the line in simulating drinking games and jumping around with swords. I can't help but smile, happy to see that they have found something exciting in *Othello,* and soon most of the audience is smiling and laughing along with me.

In the end, I give their production a B-minus, because what it offered in creativity and action it lacked in length—it was a good three minutes short of the recommended ten minutes—and fidelity to the text. When they translated the lines, the translations were rough but close; some of the lines, however, they skipped altogether. Since a full translation of the scene was a graded element of the assignment, I have to deduct some points for the patchiness of the effort.

Still, in the end I don't care. I love watching the sword fight, just as I love watching the group that brought in a pillow and blanket and turned my desk into a bed on which to stage the strangling of Desdemona, or the group that dressed in Hawaiian shirts and leis, staging their scene at a beach party.

I love watching the productions because I get to sit and let the students do the work for a while. I love watching the productions because I get to see which of my students like to ham it up, which ones have creative writing talent, and which ones are the analytic brains behind the scenes. But mostly I love watching the productions because they tell me that I have designed an assignment in which my students are demonstrating that they have learned something, and that they understand something more deeply than they understood it before.

So I sit back and enjoy myself for a couple of days and watch some *Othello*. One of the things that I realize during those two days is that I am reaping the benefits of sticking to my guns and teaching the way I know I should teach. These students are capable of getting up there and beating each other up with swords in a literature class because I pulled them out of themselves, because I made sure everyone in that class heard their voices a few times this semester, and because I maintained the sort of open, participatory classroom culture that I love and believe in.

Introduction to Literature is one of the college's general-education courses, the sort of course that students often take—and that faculty often teach—grudgingly. Of all my courses this year, I had been looking forward to this one the least. Composition is another one of those general-education courses, but there I felt I had more of a handle on the specific skill I would be teaching: writing. In my upper-level courses the skills I teach are more complex and less specific, but I have devoted my life to the study of the literature we read in those courses. Introduction to Literature offers the worst of both worlds: less specific, more complex skills and a broad range of literature with which I am not so familiar. Hence my expectations for that course were pretty low.

But lo and behold, those *Othello* productions confirm a feeling that has been creeping up on me all semester: this general-education course, the course I would never have taught at Northwestern, has become my favorite. It is the course I most look forward to teaching again, the one I am most comfortable in and in which I feel that I have made the greatest impact on my students.

It has taken me almost a full year to learn how to teach these specific students, on this specific campus, in this specific year.

But I feel as if I have finally figured it out.

(Of course, I know I will be continuing to figure it out for the rest of my career, since students and courses and the world change.)

We have one week of classes left, in which we will watch a film (*American Beauty*) and apply to it the analytic techniques we have been applying to the written word all semester. But the real climax to my first year of teaching was those days of watching *Othello*.

Film it, in fact, like this:

Shot opens on two students engaged in dialogue, against a neutral background. They might be at a party or in a dorm room. The camera slowly pulls back to reveal that they are standing in front of a blackboard, in a classroom, holding scripts from which they are reading. As the camera pulls further back, we see other actors, and swordplay and shouting begin. The voices of the actors fade and become indistinct, and now we hear tentative laughter, as if from an audience.

The camera rises and begins to turn, revealing an audience seated in a theater-style classroom, and now we see that they are students sitting relaxed at their desks, smiling and laughing in disbelief. As the camera begins to center on the middle bottom rows, we become aware of a (slightly) older adult in the room, sitting in the front row. He wears jeans and a short-sleeve golf shirt (partially untucked), dark socks and deck shoes. His legs are loosely crossed, and he laughs too. He is short-haired, balding, a day or two's beard sprouting off his jaw. He has a pencil and some paper in front of him, and occasionally he jots down a note. Mostly he just watches.

Close in on his upper frame, hold it there, and let the music begin to swell. He smiles, shaking his head a bit. His body is relaxed. He looks like a man in his element.

Housecleaning

Of course life is never like the movies, and I still have to make it through the final week and a day of classes.

My two last days of classes in my first academic year on the tenure track take place on Tuesday, May 1, and Wednesday, May 2. I have only three items on the agenda for those final days: some housekeeping items about final exams or papers, the student evaluation forms, and my parting words.

I do the evaluations first. At Northwestern I had always done the evaluations last, at the end of the final class. I would say goodbye to my students fifteen minutes before the end of class and leave them alone with the evaluations and a student I had designated to collect the forms and take them to the appropriate office.

I tried that in my first semester at Assumption and learned in my first class that it was a mistake. I had wrapped up the class, designated a student, said my goodbyes, and left for the walk across campus. Less than a minute later, when I couldn't have been more than a few hundred yards away, I turned my head just in time to see a student from that class walking out of the building.

I wanted to storm over and frog-march him back into the classroom, lecturing him about the importance of the student evaluations to his education and to me: "This is your opportunity to help me become a better teacher. This is your opportunity to improve the quality of education on this campus. This is your opportunity to improve this course for the poor kids who will be stuck with me next semester. And this is your opportunity to validate me as a teacher, to tell me how great I am, to make me feel that my hellish first semester of teaching was somehow all worthwhile, because I touched your soul in a *Dead Poets Society*–*Mr. Holland's Opus* kind of way. Do you really want to pass up all those opportunities?"

I restrained myself, but after consulting a few colleagues, I decided to prevent any future recurrence of this scenario by beginning with the evaluations, as everyone else in the department apparently does.

I go a step further and give the students a little lecture about how much the evaluations matter to me, how seriously I take them, and how much I would appreciate them spending the full ten minutes I will allot for the evaluations—during which time I will wait in the hall—giving me feedback on what we have done this semester. I emphasize that while the numerical ratings on the form are useful, the most helpful elements for me are their written comments, so I especially hope they will take the time to provide full comments.

In all four classes, they are finished with the forms and chatting with one another when I return after ten minutes, which makes me doubt the efficacy of my speech. But at least I know that everyone filled out the form, however cursorily.

After the evaluations, we attend to housekeeping matters. In my Introduction to Literature classes, I review the format of the final exam and give the students some study tips. In the Postcolonial Literature class and Argument and Persuasion, I remind them about the required elements for their final papers and answer a few questions. In no class does this take more than fifteen minutes, which means I have plenty of time for the final activity and speech I have planned.

The two most important days of the semester, I had come to believe during my time at the Searle Center, were the first and final days. The first day should stir students' intellectual curiosity about the subject matter of the course; the final day should help them process what they have learned and raise some final questions to encourage their continued interest in the subject.

I made an ambitious hash of my first day of the fall semester and now firmly believe that one ought to slide gently into those very first days of teaching as a newly hired assistant professor. But this semester I really did make use of the first day, and I believe that the dialogues I opened up with the students on that first day made a substantial difference to the quality and quantity of the contributions they made throughout the semester.

For this final day, I have planned a writing exercise that will ask them to describe what they have learned in the course, followed by a stirring and impassioned speech from me about the importance of writing as a way of thinking and learning, and about the value of literature in shaping the human soul.

But in the end—and this will come as no surprise—I'm too damn tired to do anything but wish them well and say goodbye. After we finish the course housekeeping in Argument and Persuasion, I can see them waiting expectantly to be dismissed, their hands straying towards their backpacks on the floor, their feet inching backwards as they prepare to push back their chairs and bolt. So I cop out. I thank them for their understanding and their patience with me this semester, especially during my illness, and send them on their way. One of the men shakes my hand on the way out, but otherwise we have no tearful farewells.

The other three classes wind up in the same way. I feel guilty about it— but only a little guilty. It has been a long semester and a long first year, and I think I deserve a break on this one. I'll stick to my guns next year, I think to myself, and really send them out with a pedagogical bang.

So classes end, on a Wednesday, and I have one day off before my first final exam that Friday. This will be the first final exam I have ever given in my teaching career. I have always taught either writing courses or upper-level literature courses, and for those classes I have always assigned final papers instead of exams. Since those courses always emphasized taking time to write and revise, or looking closely at texts in a specific field to construct complex interpretations, testing in limited-time format didn't really seem appropriate.

But my purpose in Introduction to Literature has been to teach students a specific set of basic interpretive skills, and it seems to me that they should be able to demonstrate those skills in an exam. I construct the exam with three parts: in the first section they have to define and give examples of various literary terms we have used throughout the semester; in the second they have to answer short essay questions on works we have read; and in the third section, to my mind the most important one, they have to write a short interpretive essay about a poem they are seeing for the first time.

"The only way for you to prepare for that question," I told them in response to somebody's question about it on the last day of class, "is to have been sitting here in class every day paying attention to how we used interpretive tools to construct meaning in works of literature."

They seem taken aback by this portion of the exam, and I wonder if I am the only instructor in the department who includes this sort of question on an exam. But as far as I am concerned, the only way to tell whether they have actually learned anything of value is to test the skills in an entirely new situation. No one is ever going to ask them at a company meeting to explain the meaning of a Philip Larkin poem, and I am enough of a realist to know that most of them will never in their lives read another poem. Given that, I still want my course to have been useful to them. In all kinds of life and work situations we are called upon to read and interpret documents or pieces of writing, and when my students find themselves in those situations, I hope they will be able to draw upon the skills they learned in this class.

I place this emphasis on skills over content especially in the Introduction to Literature course because it fulfills a general-education requirement for the college, and it seems to me that general-education courses *should* focus on skills rather than content. But in the writing and the literature courses, which are electives for majors and which focus on specific content areas, I fall back on my standard practice of assigning a final paper, with a due date halfway through finals week to give me a few extra days of grading time.

My intention is to have all those first final exams, taken on the Friday that opens finals week, graded by the time the next set of papers come in on Tuesday and Wednesday afternoon. But I take the weekend off from grading, and on Monday and Tuesday my days fill up: a doctor's appointment; a barbecue for the English honor society at Ed's house on Monday afternoon; an end-of-the-year celebratory lunch at the local café and bookstore to which I have been invited by a group of colleagues in various disciplines; a meeting with the travel agent for a spring break trip to Ireland I am helping to plan for the following year.

(This last one was a complete gift from Ed, who had organized a trip to England the year before I arrived and invited me to help him chaperone the trip to Ireland next year. We are working with a travel agency that gives us a free chaperone trip for every ten paid students, a standard deal for these group tours—and a great opportunity for faculty who love to travel and don't object to a little responsibility for minding students on the trip.)

By the time I give my second final exam, which takes place one week after the first, on the last Friday of the final exam period, I have graded only a handful of exams and papers and have a good sixty left to go.

I know I should sit down and grade them all immediately, but somehow, so close to the end, I can't bring myself to do it. I am so exhausted, and so elated at the prospect of having no more class preparations for the next four months, that the teaching part of my brain closes its doors on me with a resounding thud, to rest and recuperate for next season, and those doors stay firmly shut no matter how hard I pound on them. So for the following week—grades are not due until the second Monday after my last final exam—I grade just a few papers a day in the morning, picking up Madeleine at daycare in the early afternoon. I spend the rest of my available time working on the creative nonfiction book project about my illness that I have begun, writing in the mornings and evenings when I have the time and energy.

On Saturday of that week, two days before grades are due—senior grades were due earlier in the week, but I had almost no seniors this semester—we have commencement, and I go. As with just about every other extracurricular event I have attended this year, I am not sure whether I am supposed to attend, whether it is merely a good idea to attend, or whether it is completely voluntary. Mark and Ed are going, and I look for them in the gymnasium where we are lining up for the procession so that we can sit together.

Even though I didn't participate in the ceremonies of my Ph.D. commencement, my parents bought me the gown and hood as a graduation present. Reflecting the colors of Northwestern, my gown is a vibrant royal purple, and I definitely stand out among my mostly black-gowned colleagues. A handful of others have their own gowns as well, in their school colors, so fortunately I am not the only splash of color in this drab ceremonial sea. I do feel a little self-conscious, as if I were showing off in my fancy robes or something, but my colleagues' remarks about it are mostly good-natured.

Commencement is long and boring. The speaker is a poet who spends most of his address expressing surprise that anyone would ask him to be a commencement speaker. By the end of his speech, we're all wondering the same thing. He finishes with a beautiful poem that contains a few lines about making lunch for his child, though, and it almost redeems the event for me, since I am the lunch-maker for the children in my house. Afterwards my colleagues and I parade out of the tent between the ropes that restrain the camera-toting parents.

"Why is your gown purple?" a woman calls out to me.

"Because I'm smarter than everyone else," I say. A few of my colleagues in the line laugh, and I smile at her, to let her know it's a joke. I turn to give her the real explanation, but the procession pushes me forward and I don't have the chance.

The college has set up a reception area on the steps of the campus center, with punch and cookies, and I mill around for a few minutes, looking for people I know. But I don't see a single familiar student face. I taught only a handful of seniors this year, and the chances that I would run into one of them, in a crowd of two thousand, are small. I exchange a few words with some colleagues I know only vaguely, stand around feeling stupid for a few more minutes, and finally decide to leave. It has been a decidedly anticlimactic ceremonial finish to my first year.

(Commencement ceremonies will become more interesting and gratifying in future years, as students I have known for two, three, or four years graduate and I have the opportunity to say goodbye to them and to meet their parents and siblings. Unless you teach classes full of seniors, your first-year commencement may feel a little hollow, as everyone celebrates a class of students whom you have hardly met.)

On Sunday I finish up the dozen or so exams and papers I have left, in time to turn in my final grades by noon on Monday.

That afternoon I relax with the kids. In the evening I walk down to a neighbor's house and sit in on a meeting of the Community Service Committee of the parish council of the Catholic church we attend. My neighbor chairs the committee. My daughter occasionally plays with his daughter, and I agreed to come to the meeting when he called me about it the other night. I meet some new people, both neighbors and people from outside our neighborhood, and learn about some of the annual events the parish holds to raise money and create community among its members.

I would probably not have agreed to come to such a meeting during the semester, but now, with the vista of summer opening before me, I am happy to take advantage of an opportunity to become a more active part of a community outside the college. Anne and I have been talking about trying to become involved in such communities; she attended a recent PTO meeting at Katie's kindergarten.

So much of my time seems focused on the college, even my free time: we go to the college basketball games, we swim in the pool at the recreation center, and we hang out with my colleagues. But we also want to connect with our neighborhood and our city. I have joined this church committee, Anne will become involved in Katie's school, and we have both signed up for fall-semester classes in drawing and painting at the Worcester Art Museum.

Looking back on the satisfaction I got from those extracurricular activities, I am convinced that it would have been worthwhile to find, early on in the year, some small way to connect with a local community, in some form: church activities, local politics, art lessons, groups focused on hobbies or sports. Time spent in off-campus communities, like time spent dealing with illness or tragedy, helps you keep the tenure track in perspective.

Even after I have turned in my grades, I believe—mistakenly, it will turn out—that I am not yet finished with the college for the year. I am supposed to have a first-year review, in which the chair of my department and the dean of the college will report on their observations of my classes and recommend whether or not I should continue along the tenure track. This meeting has been on my mind for a while, and I keep expecting to receive a phone call from the dean's or provost's office to schedule the meeting.

When I ask the departmental secretary about it, she has no idea. I mention it to Mark and learn that he has been wondering about it too but has no more information than I do. An e-mail exchange with the chair, in late May, finally informs me that the meeting will not take place until September.

I'm a little disappointed. I want to know how I have done, and I would prefer to hear about it *now*, while I still remember what I have done, than when I am overwhelmed by the first weeks of a new semester. I remember reading an article at the Searle Center on student evaluations of their teachers that suggested that teachers were most likely to make improvements to their teaching if they received the feedback immediately after the semester was over (in the same way that students are more likely to make improvements to their writing if they receive prompt feedback). This makes sense to me. For the first few weeks after the semester, despite my best attempts to repress them, my courses still linger in my mind. I'm sure they will be buried irretrievably deep in my brain by the time I get to that first review.

I am especially curious to hear what the chair and the dean have to say about the classes of mine that they observed in the spring semester. Those had proved to be two very nerve-wracking classes. Even though I have confidence in my teaching skills, and even though I knew in advance which class sessions they would observe, and even though I prepared more thoroughly for those sessions than for any others the entire semester, I still had mixed feelings about being observed.

I disliked it for several reasons. First of all, it changed the dynamics of the classroom. In a classroom like mine, which relies so heavily on student participation, the shy students sometimes clam up if they see a stranger in the room. And that put me on edge because I wanted to make sure that those class days were representative ones. One bad class day could give an observer a completely false impression of my teaching. Also, like most people, I don't like the idea of someone in power making judgments about me. I went into this business in part because I like my autonomy, and I hate to be reminded that I am not in complete control of my classroom and my destiny at the college.

On the flip side, though, I am glad someone observed me because I do want to find out whether I am doing things right in the eyes of the administration. This is a strange business, as my father, an accountant and onetime CEO, occasionally reminds me, in which performance reviews are few and far between. We receive ratings from our students twice a year, but students don't make the ultimate decisions about our fates. I will receive no feedback from anyone above me—chair, dean, provost—about my job performance for *twelve months*. That is a long time to dig away in the ditch on your own, not knowing whether you are digging deep enough or in the right direction.

Institutions of higher education get away with this because they expect that people who have committed themselves to multiple-year degree programs, for such small pay as a reward, must have so much internal drive and professional commitment that they need little supervision. They also probably believe—and most of us would agree—that all those years of apprenticeship (and poverty) we suffered through in graduate school have earned us some autonomy.

And while I do agree with that in principle, at the end of my first year I am a little desperate for someone to pat me on the back and tell me I'm doing a good job—or, slightly less preferable but still better than nothing, how I can do better.

I feel like one of those high-achieving, often annoying students who are always coming into my office seeking feedback on their work, hungry for information about their status in class. I can definitely empathize with the precocious student Lisa Simpson who, in a *Simpsons* episode in which the teachers go on strike, begs her parents to please, for God's sake, *grade her* on something.

But it looks like I won't be getting my report card until September.

So instead of reflecting thoughtfully on my performance throughout the year, I spend a handful of hours a week cleaning up my office during the final weeks of May. I take all of my graded final exams and papers from the semester and stick them in a file cabinet drawer (we are required to keep final exams and papers for at least a year—I'm not sure why). A few students have given me envelopes to mail them their final papers, which I do. I had intended to give these student full written responses to their papers, but I didn't get around to it. Instead, I just made penciled notes to myself in the margin and wrote three or four phrases on the final page to help me remember why I gave the paper the grade I did. Not a single student from the first semester came and picked up his final paper at the beginning of the spring semester, so I'm not wasting time writing long comments on papers that will sit in my file cabinet for the next year or two. It made grading those final papers and exams move much more quickly than the papers I graded during the semester.

The bigger chore is filing away the materials that have accumulated in the manila folders I used for the four courses. I have assignments sheets, lesson plans, a few writing exercises I never gave back, handouts, and overheads in a fraying folder so crammed with paper that it reminds me of George's famously overstuffed wallet on *Seinfeld.* I work slowly through each folder, putting my lesson plans in chronological order, saving the overheads and one copy of the syllabus and each handout and assignment sheet, and discarding all the rest. I have most of this information, like the lesson plans, saved on my computer as well, but I figure it's best to have hard copies just in case.

I can't help but do some thinking about my first year as I sort through my lesson plans from the second semester. I can see how my courses developed over fifteen weeks and remember what worked and what didn't, which classes I threw together because I had a million other things to do and which ones I planned in painstaking detail.

The insight that strikes me most clearly concerns the rhythm of the semester, which I can chart with much more accuracy now that I have lived through two of them.

Despite the rough opening of my first semester, the first five or six weeks of each semester have probably been the most interesting parts of the courses for me. I am meeting new students and trying out all my teaching techniques on them to see how they work with a new audience. I am seeing what direction the course is taking and what areas I need to emphasize, and this requires regular fine-tuning in the early weeks of the semester. I also have very little grading to do, especially in the first two or three weeks, which frees me up to concentrate on my teaching and on mapping out the trajectory of the course as we go.

By the sixth or seventh week of the course, I am bogged down in grading, and for those next few weeks I am mostly preoccupied with trying to stay on top of all the papers I have to turn around and still maintain the standards I want to keep in the classroom. It doesn't help that advising and course selection weeks fall into that period, sucking another twenty or thirty hours from my schedule. These weeks are difficult, no doubt, but they are so busy that I almost don't have time to complain or worry about getting it all done. I just put my head down and bull my way through.

The worst part of the semester comes around week nine or ten and lasts for the next three or four weeks. Two things occur at that point: the students get sick of me, and I get sick of them.

I get sick of them because by that point I can see who's working hard and improving, who just wants her B or B-minus and will be happy with it, and who might not make it to the end of the semester. I know which students I can count on to talk in class, and which ones I will always have to prod to open their mouths. I have identified the few students—and every class has a few—who have improved in one or two areas but continue to make the same simple errors in their writing, no matter how many times I point those errors out to them; I find this endlessly frustrating. By the tenth week of the semester, then, the students have very few surprises left to offer me, and I tend to lose a little interest in them as a class.

To which statement, if I ever articulated it to them, I am quite certain their response would be "Ditto, dude."

Because they are sick of me, too. They have patiently endured all my teaching tricks. They have expressed enthusiasm for some of the things we have done in class. They have become experts in our in-class activities: the writing exercises, the group work, the debates, the discussions, the worksheets. They have seen it all, and they have figured out that I have nothing else up my sleeve. I hear groans when I tell them to get out a sheet of paper for their writing exercises, and the students who feel more comfortable with me will even let out an occasional "Awww . . . do we have to?" I get the sense that when I finish my introductory patter and launch my first discussion question, they are all staring at me and thinking, "Is this all you got?"

But then, with just a few weeks left in the semester, something wonderful happens: the end of the course starts coming into view, and we all seem to become energized by that prospect. I start to get ideas that I want to be sure to include in the course, the students start to realize that they better pay attention if they want to succeed on their final papers and exams, and we are all struck with the awareness that this little community that we have built will be dissolving in a few short weeks.

This is the time when I wander around the classroom during the writing exercises, noticing the students I will miss. This is also the time when students will mention shyly to me, before class or as they are cramming books into their backpacks, that they will see me next semester in another course of mine they have signed up for. Of course I always have a few students in every class whose backs I will be glad to see disappearing through the door for the last time, but I generally like the majority of my students and always connect with at least one or two in each class, like Dana or Krystan or Jamie.

And I shouldn't neglect the energizing force of the prospect of break, when I will have time away from school, time to write, and time to spend with my family. The anticipation of break feels very similar to the anticipation I feel before a long-awaited vacation. I relish the unstructured time of my breaks, when I am free to work in the yard, play with the kids, do the laundry, and run errands.

Now that I can see this rhythm a little more clearly than I could while I was experiencing it, I do make one final resolution about my teaching for next year. When I planned my courses, I planned each one discretely, not thinking at all about when papers and presentations came due in one course in relation to when things came due in my other courses, or in relation to my *Chronicle* deadlines or regular service duties like advising week. This lack of foresight on my part created, during both semesters, weeks in which I had to turn around a paper from every single student in my classes within a seven-day time frame.

It seems to me I should be able to avoid that situation in the future by the simple act of cross-checking my syllabi and spacing out the assignments more evenly. I vow to think more carefully about how I can help shape the rhythm of the semester, rather than just riding it out as if I had no control over it.

But the time I spend at the office in those final days amounts to no more than five or six hours a week, maybe one or two afternoons at most. The rest of my time I spend, in pure bliss, satisfying the craving to write that I have been suppressing all semester.

Anne and Katie will be in school until the third week of June, and Anne agreed to let me send Madeleine to her daycare for five or six hours during the day so that I could write. So I drop her off in the morning at around 8:3o and pick her up again an hour or two after lunch.

I am still not certain whether the creative nonfiction writing I have been doing—my essays for the *Chronicle* and a piece I published in the alumni magazine of my undergraduate alma mater—will count towards my tenure case. (I intend to ask about this at my first-year review in September.) So I resolve to work on a scholarly article based on one of the chapters of my dissertation.

I actually set several writing goals for myself for the summer, typically (for me) ambitious ones, especially considering that we are planning over a month's worth of traveling in July and August. But I want to write one scholarly article and one conference paper, both on the same subject; I want to write a few shorter pieces of creative nonfiction, aimed at a variety of different publications, both popular and literary; and I want to make headway on the memoir about my struggle with Crohn's disease that I have been thinking about and very occasionally hacking away at since December. At the very least, I want to have three full chapters and an outline, enough material to send to a literary agent and gauge the potential marketability of such a book.

In those first few weeks of the summer, though, the more serious and daunting of those projects—the book and the scholarly articles—strike me as altogether too serious and daunting. So I write some shorter pieces, pure fluff, but they let me play around with words on paper, and shape and revise a finished product, and those are the things in this world that make me happy. For a few weeks, I think to myself, I should get to do what makes me happy. I'll start worrying in June about what I need to do to get tenure.

During the afternoons, when the kids are home and playing in the yard with their friends, I spend a lot of time sitting on the front stoop with my wife. I go up there during the day too, when I am taking a break from my writing, and watch cars drive by, cats saunter through the yard, and the neighborhood mothers pushing their babies in strollers.

I spend so much time sitting on the stoop, in fact, that the first piece of eventually published writing I produce this summer is a reflection on this very activity, a short piece of creative nonfiction called "The Art of Stoop-Sitting."

After describing the correct posture and attitude for stoop-sitting, I get to the heart of the narrative in a couple of paragraphs on the more metaphysical aspects of stoop-sitting:

> Stoop-sitting, in the end, is not really about watching the world; stoop-sitting is a way of being. When you have achieved mastery of the stoop-sitting form, you are not simply watching the world; the world passes through you on its way. A properly attuned stoop-sitter has become a sponge for being.
>
> A stoop-sitter cannot interfere in the world; he has become a part of the world. On another day he will call the police on the carload of teenagers that sped through the stop sign at the corner; on another day he will sweep those grass-clippings off the sidewalk; on another day he will have a chat with his neighbor about grubs. Today he will simply exist, a part of the great spectacle of being.

Philosophizing on the great spectacle of being, sitting on my stoop, letting the world pass through me . . . No doubt about it: it's the end of May, I'm a teacher, and summertime has arrived.

Settling In
(or Just Settling?)

Anne's first year in the Worcester public school system ends in the third week of June, and we are all home together for a couple of weeks before we set out on a cross-country jaunt to visit all our former places of residence in the Midwest. During that time I spend three or four hours each morning writing, and then in the afternoons we set up the wading pool in the backyard and hang out with the kids.

I still haven't mustered the intellectual energy to work on my scholarly articles. The prospect of paging through all the critical articles and works of scholarship I have assembled in order to top off the pile with my own small insight doesn't seem as intellectually invigorating as it did in graduate school. Strangely enough, I still enjoy reading the scholarship that others have produced, so perhaps what has really happened, though I would be reluctant to admit this to myself, is that I have lost confidence in my ability to produce valuable scholarly work.

But I am not ready to confront that prospect yet, and at any rate I have become thoroughly absorbed in the nonfiction book I want to write about my experience with Crohn's disease. I am reading books about illness and trying to produce new material of my own every day.

The book occupies my mornings; in the afternoons the kids mostly occupy me, and Anne and I spend a lot of time together. This is our first summer at home together (at the Searle Center I worked through the summers). We're enjoying it for now, although it's a bit like when you first start living with someone and you have to get accustomed to the person's quirks. We're not used to having each other around all day, every day, and our separate habits and routines are jostling against one another. I discover why we never have any ice in the freezer: Anne uses about thirty cubes in her glass and never fills the tray. She watches beer and pop cans pile up on the kitchen counter for days at a time and wonders why I can't walk them thirty feet downstairs to the recycling bin.

But we do have time to talk, and one of the things we talk about, given the year we've just had, is what the future should look like for us. All questions about the future become subsumed under the one big question we both are wondering about: Can we see ourselves living in this city for the rest of our lives?

For me the question really breaks down into two questions: Can I see myself teaching at Assumption College for the rest of my life? Can I see myself living in Worcester, Massachusetts, for the rest of my life? If the answer to either of these questions is no, then should I sweep off the very light layer of dust my CV has accumulated in a year and a half and start scanning the job ads in the fall?

Put the question another way: Are we willing to settle into this city, and am I ready to settle into this job, happily ensconced in an institution and a career? Or would staying here in Worcester, at Assumption College, just mean settling—denying ourselves opportunities to create a better life at a different institution, in a different city, with different job prospects for my wife and different responsibilities and challenges for me?

This question is not a purely theoretical one. If I do plan to return to the job market in the fall, I will need to spend some time this summer preparing my cover letter, CV, and writing samples, since I know I won't have much time to work on those extracurricular activities during the semester.

Part of me groans at the prospect of turning wearily again to the job market, so early in my ride down the tenure track. But I have always heard that the best times to search for a new job are the second, third, and fourth years on the tenure track. Going on the market in the first year of a new job paints you as a malcontent, never willing to give any institution a chance. Going on the market in your fifth or sixth year paints you as fearful about the prospects for tenure at your current institution. And I have noticed that the job prospects for associate professors, or those already with tenure, are usually slim pickings. Most ads seem to call either for assistant professors or for well-established senior faculty to fill endowed chairs and distinguished visiting professorships.

If I intend to go on the market, then, knowing that determined and qualified job seekers often need more than one try in the current job market, I should probably plan to do so starting in the fall of my second year.

So throughout the latter half of June, in my mind and in the occasional conversation with Anne, as we hack away at the bushes in the backyard and plant our vegetable garden with the children playing around us, I slowly draw up my list of pros and cons for both Assumption College and Worcester.

What strikes me immediately is that in at least one very important respect—the fact that I am spending several hours a day writing—I seem to be a rough fit with the college. On more than one occasion this spring, in conversations with senior faculty both in and outside my department, I asked people about their plans for the summer. I expected to hear about book or article projects and instead heard mostly about travel and gardening plans.

For me, time away from school—which does include my share of travel and gardening, passions I apparently share with many faculty members—primarily means time to write. And while I may still be casting around for the genre in which I feel most comfortable, I am dead certain that I will always write and publish. I need my writing the way an abuser needs his substance. When I go for days or weeks without writing, I begin to feel unsettled, as if I have lost my bearings.

But it is clear to me that my writing will not be the decisive factor in my tenure decision at Assumption College. What I do in the classroom counts for substantially more in that decision than what I do in my basement at night and on summer mornings. Even my service commitments probably count for more than any of my publications.

Since I am going to write anyway, whatever my teaching load, wouldn't it make more sense for me to work at a school that would reward me for writing? The answer seems obvious to me. Big black X in the con column.

The second major item in the con column is life in Worcester.

"New Englanders can seem cold," a former graduate school colleague had warned me when she learned we were moving here. She had grown up in New England herself. "They are very loyal to their friends and family, but it can be hard to break into their circles."

I had taken this perspective with a grain of salt. I had always lived in the Midwest and found people in the various cities there to be mostly the same. I didn't really believe that people in another part of the country could be all that different.

But my colleague was right. It *has* been hard to break into the social circles of Worcester, despite our efforts to become involved with the community, at the church and at our daughter's school. It isn't that people from Worcester shun us or won't let us join them in their reindeer games. Rather, we seem like afterthoughts to them. Neighbors mention parties or events they have attended with other people we know, without any apparent discomfort at the fact that we were omitted from the guest list. As a result, we still find ourselves spending time mostly with other transplants to the city, mostly academics, and spending time with the locals only when our children are playing together or at open community events.

It doesn't help that we live in a part of Worcester that seems in some ways unusually provincial. Two of our neighbors own houses around the corner from the homes in which they grew up, and each has siblings and their families living within a two-block radius as well. Their lack of interest in us makes perfect sense. They are surrounded by the family and friends they grew up with and have no reason to seek out new friends. Understanding this, though, doesn't make dealing with it any less depressing.

This unwillingness to welcome outsiders with open arms seems to be reflected even in the city planning. On many of Worcester's main streets, there are signs identifying the side streets but no cross-signs identifying the street you are on. New to the city and trying to find our way around, we have often found ourselves taking a turn down a street whose name we don't know, then driving for what feels like miles before we hit an intersection that tells us where we are.

But the people, and the street signs designed by them, aren't the only problem. The biggest problem for both of us is the lack of a thriving downtown. After so many years in Chicago, we miss having a downtown area in which you can walk around in the evening, sampling different shops and bars and restaurants. The main street in downtown Worcester—predictably called Main Street and occupied mostly by office buildings—

pretty much shuts down at night. There are small clusters of shops and restaurants throughout the city, but no central downtown area to provide a cultural and social anchor.

We had imagined that we would spend time in Boston, since it is only forty-five miles away and could surely provide what we were looking for in a big city. But that forty-five miles is not an easy jaunt. It means driving the Massachusetts Turnpike, and it means traffic. We are also a little daunted by Boston itself, even though it is smaller than Chicago. When we moved to the suburbs of Chicago, we returned to the big city on a regular basis because it was familiar; we had lived in the heart of it for two years. But we have never lived in Boston, and the infrequency with which we visit it makes it intimidating. Every time we go there, we get lost. We never know where to park, and we have no feel for the different neighborhoods.

(I've heard other new faculty speak of this same set of disappointed expectations. You take a job in a small town, within a one or two hours' drive of a larger, more culturally diverse city, and expect to visit that city regularly. You may make regular visits there, eventually—but probably not in your first year, for all the reasons I've been writing about.)

At bottom, the truth is that we really miss Chicago. We miss our friends, we miss being within a six-hour drive of our families, we miss going downtown, we miss Lake Michigan. I miss Wrigley Field—some friends and I had purchased season tickets for the Cubs during my final year in Chicago, and I hated giving up my share—and Anne, much more the gourmand than I, misses the almost endless opportunities for dining out. Shortly after we moved to Worcester, we read a very positive restaurant review in a local magazine. The food turned out to be unimaginative and bland, no doubt aimed at the tastes of the primarily elderly patrons. It took us a while to figure out that we had to recalibrate our restaurant review expectations: five stars in Worcester would mean maybe three in Chicago.

The problem is especially acute for Anne. I have the college, which offers me an active social and intellectual life. Almost all the faculty are transplants, so they are perfectly friendly, and of course we have shared academic interests. But the teachers in Anne's schools are mostly Worcester natives, and elementary schools don't provide the same level of social and cultural opportunities as colleges, so she has no escape from the problems we are experiencing with life in this city. She has also been frustrated by her inability to find a full-time job in the public schools right away, despite her eight years of experience, and by a long delay the school district created before giving her a full-time contract. She regularly hears nightmarish stories from her fellow teachers about how the district fires many of its new teachers at the end of the school year, leaves them dangling over the summer, and then recalls them to different schools in the fall. (Though she doesn't know it yet, Anne will endure this nightmare three times in the coming years.)

The con list looks daunting, but it does not tell the whole story. It may just be that I am now home every day doing what I enjoy most, that I am returning to health after a year of illness, and that summer is beginning to assert itself with vigor. But the pro list seems to grow every time I think about it.

First, we have a wonderful home in a terrific neighborhood filled with children. While Worcester definitely needs to grow on us and the neighbors seem chilly, our children couldn't be happier. On the short block of our street we can count more than a dozen children six years of age or younger. When the weather is nice, Katie and Madeleine's afternoons are often spent outside playing with the neighborhood children, and they love it. Being a parent means displacing a significant portion of your own desire for happiness into a desire for your children's happiness, so their joy in the neighborhood goes a long way towards alleviating our varied displeasures.

In Chicago we had purchased a house just before real estate values skyrocketed in the late 1990s. When we sold it two and a half years later— a tiny three-bedroom house in a nice suburb—we made an $80,000 profit. This good fortune meant that we could afford a house in Worcester that could probably have absorbed two of our Chicago houses. In Worcester we have four bedrooms, a finished basement, a finishable walk-up attic, and a nicely landscaped yard, and we are within walking distance of the elementary school and the local independent bookstore and restaurant. So the microcosm of our home and neighborhood compensates for the deficiencies of the Worcester macrocosm.

I also like the area outside Worcester. We can reach the ocean in an hour or two, depending upon which beach we choose. Also within easy driving distance are a wide range of cities and regions: New York, Providence, Cape Cod, the White Mountains of New Hampshire, the Maine coast. Opportunities for exploring the outdoors, an activity that had recently begun to interest me, abound across a variety of landscapes. We have yet to take advantage of all these opportunities, but they are available to us.

At the college the benefits seem even clearer. While the department does have its internal divisions, everyone maintains cordial public relationships with everybody else. Everyone welcomed me into the department warmly, and I felt—perhaps naively—that I could find my place there without taking sides in the more acrimonious disputes.

And, of course, I know that every department in every college in the land has its divisions and disputes. As a graduate student I had been a pawn in one such dispute. My first dissertation advisor, a scholar of contemporary fiction who looked with skepticism on some of the popular literary theories of the day, was treated as a pariah by many members of her department. When I was the only member of my Ph.D. class to be denied a dissertation-year fellowship, she confessed to me that her status in the department had doomed my application. I have seen nothing like this in my own department, even at its worst. The cordiality may be superficial at times, but it goes a long way towards smoothing out our daily interactions in the hallways and at departmental meetings (with the exception, of course, of that horrible April meeting).

Beyond the department, Assumption College offers benefits I am lucky to have in comparison with my colleagues at other institutions. I receive $1,500 each year to travel to conferences; a friend who was hired at a research university last year laments to me that he receives only $500. I will be using my money to attend the annual Modern Language Association conference in December in New Orleans, where I will be giving a paper based on one of my *Chronicle* columns. We are going to bring the whole family and take a discounted vacation in New Orleans, since my plane ticket and meals and the hotel room will be paid for by the school. The following March I will be helping to chaperone a group of students on a spring-break trip to Ireland, and my chaperoning role will pay my transportation and lodging costs. Anne and I both love to travel, so those opportunities matter a good deal.

I also enjoy the small-college atmosphere. At Northwestern I could walk across campus, pass many hundreds of students, and not recognize a single face. At Assumption I usually can't make it halfway across our much smaller campus without seeing several familiar faces, both faculty and students. In the fall I attended a few basketball games, for our NCAA Division II program, and enjoyed being able to walk into the gym without a ticket and cheer for our students from the courtside bleachers. I pay nothing for my campus parking sticker and can always find a spot. I can take my daughters swimming at the recreation center without cost, and we always have plenty of room to splash around. In late October the school allows the children of faculty members and the surrounding neighborhood to trick-or-treat in the student dorms the Sunday before Halloween, and my children are ecstatic to have this extra holiday. All of these perks are linked to the size of the institution and to its deliberate efforts to cultivate a comfortable, familylike atmosphere on campus.

Assumption also seems to offer me excellent prospects for a stable, long-term career. I know from conversations with my colleagues that tenure, while not exactly a given, is rarely denied to those on the tenure track (the president of the college likes to say that we should be hiring so successfully that tenure decisions are a "slam dunk"). In the past five or six years, as far as I can tell, only one person has been denied tenure. Across the city, at one of the more nationally recognized institutions where the teaching load is two courses lighter and junior sabbaticals are provided— I have heard rumors (admittedly unsubstantiated) that some 75 percent of tenure cases are turned down. I know of two colleagues, in fact, who were turned down at that institution and subsequently earned tenure at Assumption. As confident as I am in my ability to publish, I would find it difficult at a school like that one ever to shed my doubts: Have I written enough? Am I publishing in the right journals? Have I received the right reviews? Those questions would undoubtedly dog me through the first six years of my career there, and I know my response would be to work myself into an early grave, trying to guarantee my success.

At Assumption, by contrast, I am fairly confident—and this will later be confirmed at my first- and third-year reviews—that my publications in creative nonfiction will count towards meeting the college's far more flexible tenure standards. That flexibility means that I need not restrict myself to any one form of writing and can continue to explore different genres until I find the one that best suits me.

Finally, and perhaps most important on the pro side, my first year at the college has helped me recognize that it matters very much to me to be teaching at a Catholic college. It took me most of the year to figure this out, in part because the Catholicism of the college is a fluctuating and contested feature of its identity.

On one level, the signs of Catholicism are everywhere on campus. From the crucifixes in the classroom to a recent lecture the college sponsored on the achievements of Pope John Paul II, from the student religious retreats to the daily masses in the campus chapel, the manifestations of Catholicism are omnipresent. Every week I get an e-mail message from "God Online," who explains the readings for that week's mass. I see the names of my students in the student newspaper as leaders of religious retreats for their peers and for local high school students.

Most of the college's specifically Catholic programs and events, though—with the major exception of the two-course theology requirement for all students—are optional. Students who wish to take advantage of these programs may do so, and nonreligious students are free to skip them. Curious about the students' perspective on this question, in Argument and Persuasion I assigned one paper on the topic of whether the college should do more to assert its Catholic identity—requiring mass attendance, for example, or a religious retreat for all students. The majority of the students argued that the college should not attempt to force Catholicism down students' throats, since people have different levels of religious conviction. Even those students who opened their papers with statements of their own Catholic identity expressed discomfort at the prospect of the college doing more to establish a Catholic presence on campus.

The more I look into it, in fact, the more it appears to me that the Catholicism of the campus is in the eye of the beholder. The religious students go on retreats and attend mass, and the college seems appropriately Catholic to them. The students who couldn't care less about religion don't read their e-mail messages from God, don't go to church, and doze their way through their required theology courses.

The same seems to hold true for faculty members.

Because I am Catholic and have an interest in the intellectual traditions of the Catholic Church and its philosophers, the signs of Catholicism are welcoming and familiar to me. I sometimes attend the noon mass at the chapel and enjoy the quiet thirty minutes in the middle of a hectic day. The lectures the college sponsors on various religious subjects always sound appealing, even if I don't always make it to them. I like the fact that I can point out biblical allusions in the poems and stories we are reading in Introduction to Literature and can expect students to be familiar with the basic plot lines of the Christian narrative. And unlike many of my students—one of whom mentions in our class discussion that he thought they were a virus and immediately deleted them—I enjoy reading the e-mails I get from God.

Mark stands at the other end of the spectrum from me. He comes from a religious background, if a slightly distant one: he spent two years after his college graduation as a youth minister in various churches and was very active for much of his life in the southern Methodist faith in which he was raised. But during his years in graduate school his religious habits fell away, and in his first year at Assumption I can see that he doesn't share my enthusiastic interest in the Catholic identity of the college.

"I had plans to spend the summer before I came here reading up on Catholicism and the religious order of the Assumptionists," he told me one afternoon when we were talking about the upcoming meeting for new faculty about the college's mission. "But you know how those summer plans go."

Another time, when the discussion in the bar one evening turned to the priests and nuns on the faculty, a Catholic colleague in philosophy and I explained to Mark the difference between Catholic diocesan priests and those in religious orders like the Jesuits or the Assumptionists, and Mark asked a number of questions about the different religious orders and their relationship to the church and to one another.

"Wow," he said afterwards. "I feel like I did the first time someone explained to me the blue line in hockey and I actually understood it."

But Mark's unawareness of the Catholic tradition, which is a central part of the college's stated mission, has not caused problems for him here or harmed his chances for advancement in any way I can see. No one has ever said anything about it to either him or me. I am glad of this; I don't want him to feel uncomfortable here, and I am happy that I can participate actively in the Catholic life of the college without others feeling pressured to do so.

Another evening, at the bar with Ed and Mark and Tom, an economics professor, I came to a clearer understanding of why the college's Catholic identity matters so much to me. I am the only practicing Catholic of the four of us, and the rest of them have spent at least part of their careers at secular institutions. But all of them, like me, share an interest in teaching questions of values, ethics, and morals, although none of us is a philosopher by training. In our courses we might ask questions that force students to consider the ethical or moral implications of an economic theory, or we might challenge them to think about the religious or spiritual issues that a work of literature raises.

At some point in the conversation it occurred to me that we shared this common bond, and I posed this question to them: "Do you feel more comfortable here than at your graduate institution raising questions about ethics, morality, and spirituality in the classroom?"

For all four of us, the answer is immediate and affirmative. And that seems to mark the most significant difference between teaching at this college and the teaching I did at my secular graduate institution. That difference has nothing to do with my technical or formal relation to the institution. It has everything to do with my values as a teacher and my comfort with the institution.

I realized later—insights gained at the bar usually need some additional reflection—that the horizon of questions I feel comfortable asking in the classroom has expanded considerably as I moved from my graduate institution to this religious college. The courses I was teaching two years ago remained tightly focused on analyzing and processing meaning in literary texts. As I grew more comfortable in my teaching, I began to raise questions about ethics and values but always felt as if I had to do so surreptitiously. I had not heard many of those questions raised in my graduate courses. Nor had I heard them raised in the classroom by professors for whom I served as a teaching assistant.

Here I see those questions as the ultimate end towards which all of our work in analysis and process is leading. Equally important, I now feel perfectly comfortable raising questions about God and spirituality and organized religion in the classroom—topics I would not have touched two years ago.

Undoubtedly some colleagues of mine—non-Catholic or nonreligious—prefer to focus on general ethics and values, without delving into the theological questions that interest me. But we can coexist happily here. They might never consider assigning papers about the Catholic character of the college in a writing class, but they would not fault or look askance at me for doing so, and this matters a great deal to me.

With the addition of this item, starred and in bold letters, the pro column of my list of positives and negatives about Assumption definitely becomes the weightier of the two. I can see, though, that most of the entries on the pro side are benefits for me, and not for my spouse. And I know that eventually, if Anne wants out of Worcester, I will have to oblige by at least testing out the market. We have made three major moves in our lives thus far: from college to St. Louis, where we both pursued master's degrees; from St. Louis to Northwestern, where I earned my Ph.D.; and from Chicago to Worcester, for my first faculty position. The first of those moves had been for Anne; she had been granted a full scholarship to Washington University, so I tagged along and earned my M.A. at St. Louis University. The second and third moves had obviously been for me. In the balancing of our relationship, then, Anne's voice will carry more weight in determining the next professional and geographical stage of our lives.

But one last factor becomes apparent to me as I reflect on the possibility of venturing onto the market, and it convinces me and Anne both that heading out this fall doesn't make sense: frankly, I am not a very attractive candidate at this point in my career.

I would not want to leave Assumption for a comparable or heavier teaching load, which means that I would be applying for jobs with a load of three or fewer courses per semester. Any school with that sort of load expects its professors to publish in their field. The problem for me is that I am in transition between my original field of contemporary British literature and the field I am slowly becoming more interested in, writing in the genre of creative nonfiction.

Thus far I have produced very little in either field, and almost nothing during this past year. I have written nothing new in my original scholarly field, and my interest in doing so in the future wanes with each semester. In creative writing, I have my five essays for the *Chronicle* and one or two other short pieces in popular periodicals. That is hardly enough to make me an attractive candidate for positions in creative writing—especially considering that I have never taken a creative writing course, much less taught one. In fact, I have never taken a single writing course of *any* kind during my college and graduate school career.

But I will be teaching a creative writing course in the fall, one that I proposed and developed, and I am writing a book that I hope to sell to a trade press. If I envision myself ultimately moving into a position in creative nonfiction writing, those accomplishments might compensate for my lack of experience and formal training in the field. So while my prospects for a run at the market this fall seem bleak, I have hopes that eventually I can write and teach my way into credibility in that field and someday prove myself an attractive candidate.

Anne understands and agrees, and neither one of us wants me to make a lateral move that might necessitate yet another eventual move. If we move again, we want it be to a place we have carefully selected and that promises us a long-term future. So we decide that we will settle into Worcester for another year, and I will settle into Assumption College for another year while doing my best to improve myself as a candidate—both for tenure at Assumption and for positions at other schools.

Which leaves the question unsettled.

It probably goes without saying that I keep these deliberations to myself. I have never heard any faculty member on the tenure track talk openly about applying for other jobs, although by the close of my first year two assistant professors I knew were leaving Assumption for other positions. To speak openly about my interest in exploring other positions would feel vaguely disloyal, and more important—and the real reason for the silence—it could even jeopardize my career. If I announce to the world, by applying for other jobs, that I am not satisfied with my position, the colleagues who will vote on my tenure case may view me as someone who doesn't belong here and vote according to my apparent wishes. Or I can see my colleagues not inviting me to become involved in long-term projects because they fear I might leave at any time.

This unwritten rule that we must remain secretive about applying for other jobs has always seemed silly and unjust to me, given the nature of our profession. In a conversation I will have with Rebecca the following year, she will articulate very clearly what I understand now only vaguely.

"We really do make so little money and have so little freedom—in terms of jobs, geography, teaching loads, et cetera—that the chance to move up is irresistible," she will explain. "No matter how much we publish or how good we are in the classroom, most schools will never reward us for that with more money or less teaching."

Listening to her, I will suddenly remember what the director of the Searle Center once told me about how people improved their positions at Northwestern: "As far as I can tell, the only way anyone ever gets more than a cost-of-living raise around here is when they get an outside job offer."

Large research institutions, and probably some wealthy private colleges as well, are able to offer that kind of flexibility with regard to salary and workload. For the most part, however, colleges like Assumption can't afford to. I can't foresee Assumption ever granting me a lighter teaching load, or a salary out of line with my peers', or a magnificent office overlooking the campus green, as a result of my publications. It also won't close its doors in Worcester and relocate the campus to Boston or Chicago for Anne.

So that leaves me two choices: either decide that those things aren't as important to me as I thought they were and learn to appreciate the benefits of a life and career at Assumption College, or hold tight to those desires and let them drag me back onto the market.

By the end of June, we haven't agreed upon on any final or grand plan, but we have at least settled on the next year, which I'll be spending at Assumption.

Beyond that, nothing settled yet.

Affirming

Freed up for the summer, Anne and I pack up the kids and spend most of July on the road. We undertake a monumental road trip back to the Midwest that returns us to the cities we grew up in and lived in as young adults: Cleveland, St. Louis, Chicago. We are even making a pit stop in South Bend, Indiana, city of our alma maters, to ensure full coverage of our former homes.

The amount of time I spend in the car over these three weeks probably beats the amount of time I spent commuting back and forth to school during my entire first year, since we live just two miles from campus. We start with eleven hours to Cleveland. From there it's nine hours to St. Louis, then a short five-hour hop to Chicago, another six hours back to Cleveland, and the return trip of eleven hours back to Worcester. We are breaking up the longest two legs of the journey, staying overnight at hotels in nondescript cities in the middle of Pennsylvania.

The scope of the trip, and the fact that we are taking it with a five-year-old and three-year-old, is of course insane, especially given the year we have been through. If we were smart, we would spend the summer relaxing, regaining our strength, and regrouping for the next year of school. But I will discover in future years that we are participating in a ritual that many new faculty members undertake during their first significant break from the tenure track: the return trip to their previous home, the trip that finally forces them to admit that life there has moved on without them and that they now live somewhere else.

That confrontation can prove traumatic. During her first break, over the holidays of 2001–2, Rebecca will return to her home in West Virginia shell-shocked from her first semester. She steels herself to return for the second semester by telling herself that it will all be over in three months, and then she'll start a new career doing something else. When a blizzard hits just before she has to drive back to Massachusetts in January, she briefly wonders whether she should bother returning at all.

My experiences in this first year, arduous and unexpected in so many ways, have not produced a reaction that strong. I know I will be back next year. I know that next year will be better than this year, just as I know that the second semester would have been better than the first one—especially in terms of my anxiety and comfort levels in the classroom—had it not been for my illness. And I don't quite know, but I am pretty confident, that I will eventually master the challenges and resolve many (though probably not all) of the questions that were still plaguing me at the end of my first year.

Over the course of those three weeks on the road, as Raffi songs fill the minivan and we plow through the mountains of upstate New York and the flat expanses of Midwestern agriculture, placating the children with snacks and toys, alternately driving and grabbing cat naps, I have plenty of time to reflect on the year gone by and to gain some perspective on it.

As we revisit familiar haunts and old friends throughout the Midwest, including a brief stop at Northwestern, I begin to see how many new situations and complexities I *didn't* have to face during my first year at Assumption—the sort of complexities that would confront a new assistant professor in the sciences, for example, or a new assistant professor at a research university like Northwestern.

Their pressures are obviously different from mine. My younger daughter has spent the last year with an in-home day-care provider who also watches the son of a new faculty member at a more prestigious college across town. Whenever we had a few minutes together to talk, during which time we always discussed our work, he never spoke about teaching; he always focused on the pressures he felt to produce publications. He needed a published book to give him even a decent shot at tenure, and even that was no guarantee. Of course he also had the benefits of a junior sabbatical, a paid semester of leave in his third year, which certainly would help.

I know as well, from the work I did with graduate students in the sciences in my position at the Searle Center, that they face the additional challenges of obtaining grant money to support their research and of finding the physical space and equipment to start up a program. Obtaining grants is not normally a required part of setting up research programs in the humanities, but I did help out with some grant applications at the center—and I hated it. It felt like the research you have to do on potential markets for your writing: I understood that it was necessary, but it always felt like busywork, and what I really wanted was to focus on the writing itself.

Finding grant money, working with teaching assistants, producing published work at breakneck speed—I am happy to have avoided those challenges and others like them faced by my colleagues in other disciplines and at other universities. I still wonder whether some of those challenges might ultimately prove a better fit for me in my career, but I have already decided not to pursue that question any further for another year or two.

Obviously I have faced challenges of my own, those specific to small liberal arts colleges as well as those more generally faced by new assistant professors, and I am happy to have at least bulled my way through most of them. And as I look back on those challenges while enjoying my time away from Worcester, sitting in the stands at Wrigley Field or chasing my daughters around a children's museum in St. Louis, a feeling I would never have imagined experiencing three or six months ago begins to well up inside of me: I miss school.

At the end of the six weeks of writing time I had to myself in late May and early June, after the semester had finished for me but while Anne and the girls were still in school, I started to wonder whether I might not be better suited for a life of freelance writing. I found it incredibly satisfying to have my time completely to myself, to manage several writing projects at once, and to have the luxury of watching those projects progress or even come to fruition. I knew it would take several years of dedicated after-hours freelancing to build up enough outlets for my work to allow me to quit my job at the college, but I started to wonder whether I should set myself that goal and begin working towards it.

But now, away from both writing and school, I find myself being pulled in two directions. On the road for three weeks, with all my time during the day allotted to travel or children, I have no time to write, and of course I miss that. I occasionally write down ideas or little snatches of prose on a notepad I brought along with me, but it's not the same. I miss the sustained effort of creativity that an essay or a chapter demands.

But I also discover, away from the college and my colleagues and students, that I miss them as well.

That emotion helps me begin to see that with all the unexpected challenges, the frustrations, and even the illness, I enjoyed my first year of teaching. I felt liberated in being able to control my own schedule, to arrange my office hours and my free time as I saw fit. I enjoyed getting to know the students, some more than others. I felt elation at those moments in the classroom when everything was going according to plan, or when everything was not going according to plan but was still working out beautifully. I felt satisfaction that although I failed at first, I pressed on and attained some measure of success in the classroom. I enjoyed working on a college campus, with its carefully sculpted landscapes and wooded pathways, with the faces of young people all around me, and with its rich intellectual life—the only work environment in which I have ever felt truly comfortable. I appreciated the amount of time I was able to spend with my children, far more than had been available to me at the Searle Center, or would have been available to me in any administrative or nonacademic position.

And I am appreciating the *hell* out of these three months of vacation.

"The three best reasons to be a teacher," one of my wife's teacher friends joked to me at their end-of-the-year party, "are June, July, and August."

Don't forget December and January, I thought to myself but didn't say, since she didn't enjoy the same extensive winter holidays that I did.

That may seem like a trivial reason to value a job or a profession, but because my writing and my family matter so much to me, those months of freedom are important. The opportunities to write and to spend time and travel with my family would go a long way towards pulling me back to the campus every September.

But all of those reasons, ultimately, are secondary to the single most important and most philosophical motivation that will have me forever darkening the doors of college classrooms. This motivation has always lurked somewhere below the surface of my consciousness; a conversation with my brother over the July Fourth weekend helps me formulate it fully for the first time.

Tony is a political scientist, who earned his Ph.D. in international relations from Johns Hopkins University and spent a few years as an assistant professor of political science at the American University in Cairo. After four years there he and his wife wanted to return to the United States with their infant son, so Tony took a job with an international-relations think tank in New York City the same year I began my job at Assumption. He will hold this job for three years, before the academy will call him back to teaching and to a third phase of his career.

Like many other political scientists, Tony has always been interested in the real-world applications of his academic discipline, and he has contemplated taking a role in the American political arena. His job at the think tank, which involves organizing conferences and events for academics, politicians, and journalists, has given him a taste of the sort of work he might do out in the public sphere, away from the familiar environment of the college campus.

We both visit my parents' home in Cleveland during the first week of July, and he and I talk about our respective years in our new positions. He has enjoyed his job thus far and can't decide whether he should continue working in the public sphere—admittedly the somewhat rarified public sphere of the think tank—or return to the classroom.

We both have little children, and we are chasing them around the basement playroom of my parents' house as we talk about this. The conversation is crystallizing my thoughts about my place in the academy, so I am ready to answer when he finally asks me the question, "So what do you like so much about being a professor?"

"I like the fact," I say to him, "that for most of the people in my classrooms, these four years will be the last time in their lives when they really care about books and ideas. These will be the last four years when they believe that books and ideas matter, and that books and ideas can change the world, can make it a better place. Most people are too busy working for a living, doing their jobs and raising their families, to care much about that or even to believe it anymore. I understand those pressures and responsibilities and how exhausting they can be; I'm not knocking people who no longer have the time or energy for idealism. But I still believe in idealism and young people, I still believe in books and ideas, and I still believe that those things can make the world a better place. So I want to have my chance at these kids now, while they are still holding on to their ideals, and do everything in my power to encourage them to care about books and ideas for the rest of their lives."

I'm sort of surprised that this formulation has come out so clearly.

"That's a good point," Tony says, nodding his head slowly.

At that moment someone's kid cries for more juice or spills something or needs a diaper change, and the conversation ends.

Afterwards I write the thought down in one of my notebooks, because I want to remember it. And for the rest of the trip, whenever I write something else down in that notebook, I look at that thought again, and it seems truer to me each time I reread it.

I have already mentioned this tendency I have to compare my current self to my undergraduate self, and this year has helped me sort out just what in that earlier self still matters to me. I have no reason to cling to his excessive drinking, his selfishness, or his belief in the complete origi nality and brilliance of his ideas. I have long discarded his lack of re- spect for, or interest in, his physical self or the natural world. I learned last semester that he didn't know much about teaching and learning.

But I have every reason to cling to the two traits that I see now have stayed with me for the past ten years: his love of books and ideas, and his belief that he could change the world.

He believed he would change the world by writing literary novels that would bring enlightenment and wisdom to his readers. He didn't understand the realities of publishing in the late twentieth- and early twenty-first centuries. He also didn't know that any writing talent he had might not lie in the realm of fiction.

He was right about one thing, though. He may never write bestselling novels, but he will still have the opportunity to change the world, to offer enlightenment and wisdom to the hundreds and thousands of young people who will pass through his classrooms. He will still be able to hold tight to his ideals about what matters in this world, even as he watches those ideals mature into subtler and better informed perspectives on the big questions that have always interested him, the most important questions we can ask about what it means to be a human being. He will hold on to his commitment to writing, even if he can't put as many hours into it as he once had envisioned. He will still be able to live among others who share his ideals and his love of books and ideas, and who love to engage in the sort of dorm-room conversations he used to have at 2 A.M. with his roommates, sometimes sober and sometimes not, about the existence of God and the meaning of life.

And he will, I am quite certain, come to value these parts of his life and his profession so much—in spite of illnesses and bad days in the classroom and occasionally distempered colleagues—that he will dedicate the rest of his life to them.

August Redux, Beginning Again

On a warm August morning, back from my family's travels through the Midwest and starting to turn my thoughts towards the coming academic year, I hop onto my bicycle and coast down Commodore Road, which slopes down from our house to the bottom of a hill. I turn the corner onto Chandler Street, passing Tatnuck Bookseller's, the local independent bookstore and restaurant. I pedal for a half-mile up a gentle incline and turn left onto the street just past Nancy Chang's, the Chinese restaurant from which we sometimes order takeout.

I see the moving truck parked in front of a gray triple-decker a few hundred yards off the main road. I recognize Rebecca and coast up to the sidewalk. She introduces me to two graduate student friends who have driven up from West Virginia to help her move, one of whom is beginning his career as an assistant professor of English at a college in Pennsylvania much like Assumption.

We talk a bit as we move, but mostly we sweat and grunt, working Rebecca's furniture and boxes up two winding flights of stairs into the apartment she has rented for the upcoming year—a long, beautiful space with hardwood floors and bay windows in the front. She doesn't yet know that those windows will prove both a blessing and a curse, when the aroma of Chinese food wafts into her apartment on warm summer evenings.

We're done within an hour. Rebecca is single and has been living on graduate student wages, so she has not accumulated enough stuff to make moving quite the chore for her that it was for Anne and me at this same time last year. As I am leaving, I invite her to a barbecue we are having for some of our friends in the department that afternoon. She seems pleased at the invitation and promises to come.

When she arrives, we are all out on the back deck drinking beer under the shade of the massive tree that the previous homeowners built up landscaping around and condemned to a slow death; its dead or dying branches arch high above us, reaching into the neighbor's backyard. It's a warm summer afternoon, and we are lazily postponing the moment when barbecue etiquette demands that we pull ourselves off the green plastic lawn furniture and fire up the grill.

I watch Rebecca talking to her new colleagues and their spouses. She is tall and fair-skinned, with small dark glasses and long and thick red hair. Even pulled into the ponytail I will become accustomed to seeing her wear, her hair always looks to me as if it were longing for release, ready to burst from its restraints and declare its freedom.

I have become the veteran now, and I feel just the mildest bit protective of her. I want to do what I can to help her negotiate the landscape I have crossed and recrossed and am readying to cross again. I don't want to impose upon her, though, so when we talk I simply state my availability to help her in any way I can, and especially—given that we are only weeks away from the start of the semester—in preparing her syllabi, planning her classes, or just finding her way around the department, the college, and the neighborhood. She asks a question or two but otherwise seems pretty self-sufficient and ready for the semester.

I wish I had time to give her all the information I would have liked to have had at the beginning of my first semester, but I have kids and a book project and the semester is starting for me, too. I'll help her out when I can, the way my colleagues helped me out when they could.

But even if I could at that moment present her with this book I am two years away from writing, it still wouldn't prepare her for every twist and wrinkle that will complicate her passage through that first year. Like everyone else, she must forge her own path.

But I will help her, I know, as I hope this book will help readers who are in her position—or hoping to be in her position someday—as they read it. At the very least I can help her by telling her that her traumas were my traumas too, and perhaps even the traumas of every first-year professor. I know from my writing and reading about chronic illness that sometimes the best help you can provide to someone confronting a difficult and life-changing experience is simply to show them that others have swum in this same ocean whose icy waves they imagine they are the first to furrow. I think I can help her too in negotiating her way through the department and its service obligations, in setting realistic goals for her writing and research, and in identifying concrete techniques that will make her more comfortable and successful in the classroom.

But I know too that she will survive that first year the way we all survive it: barely treading water, getting her head above the surf just in time to see the next wave of papers come crashing down, wondering whether she is doing it right and what she has got herself into. And searching for, and occasionally finding, those moments of elation and triumph—in the classroom, in the office, in the library or at the writing desk, at a poetry reading or a lecture, at a conference, even in a meeting—that draw all of us to the life of the mind, that make it all worthwhile, and that have led me to this moment of contentment, on a weekday August afternoon, eating and drinking and laughing in the sun with my colleagues, anticipating the year to come.

Resources for First-Year Faculty
A Brief Annotated Selection

With the exception of the first, very recent one, all of the sources listed below are ones that I consulted regularly during my first year at Assumption. Most of them I discovered while I was at Northwestern. I recommend them all highly to first-year professors in any discipline.

Print Resources

> Bain, Ken. *What the Best College Teachers Do.* Cambridge: Harvard University Press, 2004.

Until this past spring, I would have had to say that the resource that proved most helpful to me during my first year was not available to the general public. I would have said that no single resource could compare with the time I spent under the tutelage of Ken Bain, who served as director of Northwestern's Searle Center for Teaching Excellence during my three years as assistant director, and who now serves as director of New York University's Center for Teaching Excellence. For the past fifteen years Ken has been conducting a long-term, qualitative study of the most successful teachers at colleges and universities, analyzing their practices and characteristics both in and outside the classroom. While I served at the center, I spent some time helping with that study, and I learned more from my interactions with Ken and from the teachers he studied than from any other resource.

Fortunately, Ken Bain now comes in book form. The results of his study were published in the spring of 2004. This book comes as close as possible to providing the terrific insight into teaching that I was able to obtain firsthand from the author.

McKeachie, Wilbert, et al. *McKeachie's Teaching Tips: Strategies, Research, and Theory for New College and University Teachers.* Eleventh ed. Boston: Houghton Mifflin, 2002.

Before Ken Bain's book came around, this would have been the one book I recommended to all new faculty. We used to purchase copies of it for all new faculty members at Northwestern and distribute them at the New Faculty Orientation. The book covers just about every area of teaching you can imagine, from lecturing and grading to managing classroom space. Each piece of practical advice about teaching is supported by extensive pedagogical theory and research, described in brief and easily understandable terminology.

Originally authored solely by Wilbert McKeachie, the book is now in its eleventh edition and features contributions from a variety of other experts on higher-education pedagogy.

Frederick, Peter. "The Dreaded Discussion: Ten Ways to Start." *Improving College and University Teaching* 29 (Summer 1981): 109–14.

This article was my holy text for my first few years of teaching, beginning at the Searle Center. I have tried every one of these ten ideas, with varying degrees of success. But by the end of my first year at Assumption I had settled on a handful that worked extremely well for me and my students, and I still use those techniques frequently. If you want to run your classroom by discussion, if you want to avoid conventional question-and-answer sessions, or if you want to revitalize your discussion classroom, find and read this article; it has been widely reprinted. The suggestions are specific, innovative, and effective.

Bruffee, Kenneth A. "Consensus Groups: A Basic Model of Classroom Collaboration." In *Collaborative Learning: Higher Education, Interdependence, and the Authority of Knowledge.* Baltimore, Md.: Johns Hopkins University Press, 1993.

Bruffee's book as a whole is excellent, and this chapter in particular has proven the most useful to me. Bruffee proposes a specific model for structuring classroom activity, one that involves working with students in groups. While I don't believe I have ever implemented Bruffee's exact model, the reasoning behind it proved enormously helpful to me in thinking about what discussion can and should accomplish in the classroom.

The Chronicle of Higher Education

I started reading the *Chronicle* at the Searle Center, since we subscribed to it there. I continue to read it whenever I have the time—though I will confess I had the time infrequently during my first year. The *Chronicle* won't usually provide concrete tips on how to conduct your academic life, but it will make you an informed citizen of the academic world. No other source provides such a broad and current perspective on the enterprise of higher education in the United States.

Online Resources

The Chronicle of Higher Education: Chronicle Careers. http://chronicle.com/jobs

The online job section of the *Chronicle* has long been a useful resource for job-hunters in academe, but these days it offers much more and is read by many academics other than job-seekers. You will find the job ads there, of course, but now you will also find a host of both occasional and regular columnists writing about every aspect of academic life, from serving as a dean or a chair to surviving both adjunct and tenure-track careers, from research and publishing to serving on committees and combining academic life with parenting. If it pertains to academic life, you will find a column about it somewhere on this site.

My favorites are the regular columns by Ms. Mentor (who is channeled by Emily Toth of Louisiana State University at Baton Rouge) and Stanley Fish (who still hasn't called).

Tomorrow's Professor Listserv: Desktop Faculty Development, One Hundred Times a Year. Moderator Rick Reis, Stanford University. http://ctl.stanford.edu/Tomprof/index.shtml

A Stanford engineer, Rick Reis established this listserv after publishing *Tomorrow's Professor: Preparing for Academic Careers in Science and Engineering* in 1997. The listserv he created, which sends out messages twice a week on a wide variety of topics—from practical teaching tips to new research in higher education—expanded to address academic issues and questions from all disciplines. Postings to the listserv are almost always excerpts from books on higher education, so the list both provides tips and informs subscribers about new books in the field.

www.jamesmlang.com

Visit the author's web site for more resources on surviving in academe—including a full archive of the author's columns from *The Chronicle of Higher Education*—and for more information on the book and the author's path to tenure.